I AM A RETIRED ATHLETE...

WHAT NOW ?

JANAE WHITTAKER ALI

Foreword by Drew Bledsoe

I am a Retired Athlete...What Now?

The Five Secrets of Winning in Life Beyond Sport

Written By: Janae Whittaker Ali

Edited By: Peggy Paul Casella

Formatted By: Russell Ali

Cover Design by: Shelley Futch Anderson

Cover Photo by: Jim Hontz

Cover model: Janae Whittaker Ali

ISBN- 13: 978-0-9986924-0-1
ISBN- 10: 0-9986924-0-9
LCCN- 2018907404

Give feedback on the book at: Transitionwhatnow.com

First printing edition 2018 / Printed in the United States of America

Table Of Contents

Post to our social media pages at:
Instagram.com/transitionwhatnow
Facebook.com/transitionwhatnow

Acknowledgment

I want to thank my career ending knee injury. Without you I would not have gone through the depth of struggle with retiring from sport; which brought forth my awareness that the struggle is out there and the support is not.

Thank you to the celebrity and college athletes I interviewed as well as Drew for your foreword. Your contribution will support, comfort and inspire many athletes.

Thank you to my Mom and Dad for graciously supporting my gymnastics career and letting me lead the way.

Lastly, thank you to my husband who rode most of this retirement ride with me and has been nothing but supportive and excited about my work.

Foreword

Facing retirement from a sport is a daunting task. As a professional football player it was especially daunting. Outside observers have little sympathy for those of us who have been blessed to get paid to play a game (nor should they, it is an amazing blessing!). That doesn't change the fact that there are some unique and difficult challenges we face. Most successful career paths require years and years of climbing through the ranks to achieve status and financial stability. Most successful careers also have a longer lifespan than professional sports and if you face corporate transition you can usually find a similar position in another company. If you are a retired NFL offensive lineman it's awfully hard to find another job where you're required to push giant men around for a living. The statistics clearly show that transition in sport can be problematic. That is why this book is so important.

I have found that many of the skills I used as an athlete have been applicable in my second life. Those same skills were important in my transition. Skills like planning, practice, work ethic, perseverance and leadership can all be applied to your next phase in life; if you take the time and use resources like Janae's book to figure out how to best implement them.

Planning – We always had a game plan going into a game right? I developed a plan fairly early in my football career for my next phase (very few athletes do this). The plan, however, was far from perfect and has continued to evolve but at least I had a plan to work from.

Practice - None of us arrived at athletic success without years and years of practice. We can't expect to be successful immediately in our next phase.

Work Ethic - Remember, when we start our next phase of life we are rookies again. Sometimes you have to grind it out [again] to become successful once more. None of us had it handed to us in sports. Why should we expect the next phase be any different?

Perseverance - There will be setbacks. There were setback in sports. To expect everything in the second phase to go completely smooth is foolish. Embrace the inevitable challenges and take pride in working through them.

Leadership - One thing I've found to be very rewarding is leadership. The platform we have as athletes is powerful. We can make a huge difference, particularly in the lives of young people. The magic part of choosing to utilize our platform is that it can also give us great feelings of empowerment and satisfaction. Every time I have had the opportunity to work with young people I've come away feeling like I gain more than I gave.

Please take the time to read through this important book. We have been given a head start in life through sports. We all need to make sure we capitalize on this head start seeking guidance instead of pridefully attempting to get through this hard time alone and find ourselves going backward.
Go Cougs!

Drew Bledsoe
WSU QB, No. 1 NFL draft pick, 14 year NFL QB for the Patriots, Bills and Cowboys

Chapter One

Warm up

I authored this book six years after facing the harsh unexpected struggle with no longer being a competitive athlete; and realizing I was not alone. The book never felt fully complete. I spent the next few years gaining wisdom- getting married, deepening my faith, having kids, growing my business with current athletes and beginning my masters degree. I felt the nudge to continue with this work. The time was right to step forward in support of many athletes out there who need to figure out what is next without sport defining their life.

I have gone through involuntary retirement, gained wisdom and have come out balanced, on purpose and thriving.

There is a lot of work to do, and everyone's journey is their own. You are accustomed to that in being an athlete. If you feel a bit off path, lost or unsure about your future without sport, this is for you. If you stay awake at night plagued with the "what ifs" of your career, or are haunted by dreams of unresolved athletic endeavors, this is for you. If you just want to make the best of the incredible skills you have; I am excited to see how this book helps you get back on top of your life. Back to winning, back to a life of meaning.

This book is designed to get the large ball rolling. No news to a star athlete like yourself; you will get out what you put into it. If you skim the words, you may catch a nugget you need. But if you devote yourself to this training for the sport of life, do the exercises, take the time to watch the movies and earn the points, your life will be on a very different trajectory than now.

This work is intended for overall healthy people who need support taking life to the next level. It is not intended for those with mental illness, addictions or other psychological issues. Please seek professional help and come back to this program when you are ready.

It may help to pick a consistent time to devote to this (e.g. first thing in am, lunch hour, before bed, Saturdays). If you don't have room to write everything with space provided, use margins or your own paper/computer.

Also, I suggest having a fellow athlete go through this with you. It will give you a sounding board, equip you with built in accountability and helping others– helps yourself!

Throughout the book, you will see "**Share Opp**" (sharing opportunity). I invite you to share in the online community to gain support, generate momentum, have accountability and inspire others. You will also practice focus and discipline– do not allow yourself to get distracted on social media.

Post to our social media pages at:
Instagram.com/transitionwhatnow
Facebook.com/transitionwhatnow

As athletes, you have acquired the tools to win. All of us were meant to do life, side by side. Swallow any pride and get excited to thrive.

Chapter Two

Getting Started

Congratulations on suiting up for another big game - your life!

It may be hard to believe, but there are games to win in life after sport, too.

If you are like I was after a severe knee injury ended my career, you may not have thought about retirement in that way. Even though you knew in the back of your mind that you would face retirement someday, you may not feel fully prepared for what you actually face in this transition today.

In your life beyond sport you may be feeling lost—the "Who am I and what do I do now?" syndrome. You may feel like something is missing, or that any new venture isn't quite the same as being an athlete. You might feel unfulfilled, bored, depressed, lost, confused, or nostalgic. "Retirement from sport, especially when it is unplanned, has been referred to as a social death. [1]"

If your retirement was not by choice, chances are you weren't ready for the "glory days" to end. You had unfinished business. Perhaps you did not accomplish everything you set out to do, or maybe you made it to the top of your game and were just about to reach that lifelong goal, and now your career is over; suddenly you are no longer an

---

[1] [1]. 1. Baillie, P. H. F., & Danish, S. J. Understanding the career transition of athletes. Sport Psychologist, 1992. p 6.

athlete.

When the initial shock settles, you probably find it hard to imagine being anything other than a prized athlete. Even if it was planned there may be loss and tough transition ahead. And even if you were burned out at the end of your career, transition may still prove challenging.

The bottom line is that for as long as you can remember, your life has been about training to excel in sport, and now that sport has fallen out of the equation, you have some re-evaluating to do. You realize that you miss the team aspect, the recognition, the structure, the goals, the encouragement, the meaning, and, of course, the rush of game time!

Athletes who have a love for their sport may avoid dealing with the sudden transition, and that may play out in many ways:

- A series of unfulfilled jobs.
- Trying to stay involved in your sport (competing or coaching) to hang on as long as possible, because it is all you know.
- Buying time to avoid the "real world" by getting an advanced degree or something similar even though you don't yet know what you want to do.
- Reckless behavior.

One sport in which retirement has been studied more extensively is professional football. Ken Reuttgers of Gamesover.org found that of players who retired from the NFL:

- 25% are bankrupt one year after retirement
- 50% of all divorces occur within the first year after retirement
- 65% lack a college degree and marketable job skills
- 78% are bankrupt, divorced, or unemployed two years after leaving the game
- 100% of players will experience career termination[2]

While the NFL has increased focus on player development for active players, that support seemingly diminishes once the players are out of the game. But does that mean all retired players are destined for bankruptcy, divorce, unemployment, and other negative outcomes? Absolutely not.

"The literature suggests that problems arise when career transition is involuntary. Mihovilovic (1968) contends that athletes may have no control over their retirement because of injury, being cut, conflict with management, or family reasons. Injuries and health problems often play a negative role in the career transition of athletes. Those who face injury are often unable to control when and how the retirement process transpires (Werthner & Orlick, 1986), and career-ending injuries often do not allow athletes to accomplish their goals and plans for life outside of sport. Athletes who are involved in involuntary retirement are often more resistant and less prepared than are those who retire voluntarily (McPherson, 1980)."[3]

Whether your retirement was voluntary or involuntary, one thing is certain: if you were dedicated to your sport, you will

[2] Reuttgers, Ken. Www.Gamesover.org. Retrieved June 2006. (Site no longer available).
[3] . Hayman and Andersen. Journal Of Excellence. Issue #13. 2009 (McKnight et al).

experience grief and loss without it—including physical, social, spiritual, emotional, and mental consequences.

Share Opp- @transitionwhatnow post your reason for retiring and #newseason.
- **Injury**
- **Contract ended**
- **Graduation**
- **Moving on**
- **Other**

Tim Ferriss (putting it bluntly) in his bestselling book- *The Four Hour Work Week*, defines characteristics that separate the "New Rich." Instead of a desire to have more, the New Rich desire to, "Have more quality and less clutter. To have huge financial reserves but recognizes that most material wants are justifications for spending time on the things that don't really matter, including buying things and preparing to buy things. You spent two weeks negotiating your new Infinity with the dealership and got $10,000 off? That's great. Does your life have a purpose? Are you contributing anything useful to this world, or just shuffling papers, banging on a keyboard, and coming home to a drunken existence on the weekends?"[4]

In a recent study, researchers interviewed athletes "...in their early- to mid-twenties who had competed at the elite level. They found that their retirement followed one of three courses: *Entangled, Going Forward* or *Making Sense.*"[5]

---

[4] Ferriss, Timothy. The 4-Hour Workweek: Escape 9-5, Live Anywhere, and Join the New Rich. Crown Publishing Group, 2007. p21.
[5] Marquette, Terra. Study: Retired Athletes Struggle With Loss Of Sports Culture, Finding New Identity. Happiness, Psychological, Sports. February, 28, 2018.

Without even reading further descriptions, I am sure you can relate.

I designed this "What Now?" book to support you through this period and to launch you into a *purposeful winning life* beyond sport...going forward.

Think of this as your new playbook for creating a life beyond sport that is even more rewarding and glorious than your life as an athlete. If you cannot even fathom this concept, you are in the right place. You will discover true glory and fulfillment beyond anything a gold medal or championship ring can bring. Athletes at all levels, sports, and backgrounds have been successful in life beyond sport. I have interviewed many celebrity athletes and I am going to share some secrets with you—including my own story.

This is a workbook. It is not designed for you to sit back, read, and hope for some insight. Insight is powerful, but insight without action is inconsequential. You must be ready to get into action.

The great news is that, after you work your way through this book, you will no longer be saying, "Life as an athlete was as good as it gets." You have your whole life ahead of you, no matter your age. There is no point in living with the mindset or perception that it will never be better than the past. That is a very common misconception among athletes. *Gear up—your greatest wins are ahead of you!*

Most athletes have based their personal significance on praise and status, and for this reason it is hard to imagine fulfillment without it. It was for me even as a collegiate gymnast. But as Charles Colson says, "Living a life of significance does not depend on the prerogatives that belong to high position; it depends even less on others' esteem and praise. Living a meaningful life consists simply in embracing the responsibilities and work given to us, whatever they are."[6] It will take some work to deconstruct a dependency on esteem and praise. This book will help you with that, with the focus on getting you to lace up your boots and get out there. A trait so great about athletes is that you already have the drive to work and win!

The best part about being an athlete—retired or not—is that not only do you have the drive to win, but you are also physically **designed for greatness!** Like a car is designed to drive, you are designed for greatness; you have proven you are willing to make sacrifices and do what it takes.

As you trained in your sport, you accomplished much more than skill acquisition. **"Dedicating your life to training was really dedicating your training to life."[7]**

Here is an illustration of how you are designed for greatness. Think of the first time you learned a new motor skill or play in your sport (e.g., a new jump, throw, play, shot, style, twist, or flip). The first time you did this maneuver it seemed awkward, slow, and choppy. With repetition it became easier and easier to complete the skill or play. Then you could add some flair to it, and eventually you felt like you could do it in your sleep.

As a young gymnast, I remember learning a back handspring

[6] Colson, Charles. The Good Life - Seeking Purpose, Meaning and Truth in Your Life. Carol Stream, Tyndale, 2006.
[7] Millman, Dan. Interview. 2005.

(a back bending flip with hands touching) on balance beam. It was awkward, hard, and extremely scary. I first had to learn how to safely perform it on the floor. Years later, as I perfected my motor skills, I learned to perform it along a straight line on the floor, being very sure to keep my hands on the line. If I didn't learn to keep my hands on that line, progressing to high beam with my hands apart would result in, well, flipping backwards onto my head!

After mastering a back handspring on the line, the next steps were bringing it to the low beam with mats on the side, perfecting that, then taking away the mats, then moving to the medium beam, and finally taking it to the high beam—again with mats to start. At each stage of the process, it seemed like a whole new skill all over again.

When I was learning this skill on high beam, I wasn't allowed to leave the gym until I practiced it. I would dread the moment all through the workout, if not the entire school day, knowing what was to come (I am sure you can relate to dreading a practice, drill, or opponent). But every time I completed a successful back handspring, I was connecting more and more neurons (nerve cells), which were telling my body how to execute this skill. Creating neural pathways is how habits form, both good and bad.

The goal is to repeatedly execute the skill until it is no longer scary or difficult. I began perfecting my ability on high beam to the point where I could execute a back handspring in competition, confident I would stay on the beam. This move became so natural that I soon started adding connecting flips and jumps.

There are several training tools for life in this. The awkwardness and inability to do the skill in the beginning did not become a brick wall that I couldn't get past, but a hurdle to get over. I may have failed a few times, but I kept going. I progressed. I received feedback from my coach, implemented it, and I eventually began perfecting the skill. I listened to my coach and made the necessary shifts. And all the while, my nervous system was carving and memorizing the technicalities of this movement.

We each have had this experience in our sport, on different stages and with different skills. The ability to do a back handspring is just one of the hundreds of skills I learned as I attempted to master the art of winning. Although athletics is obviously not the only arena that practices winning, it is a large focus in sport. To be clear, though, when I say "winning," I am not referring to competition, or the comparison between you and other athletes; I am referring to doing your best and reaching your highest potential.

In your sport, winning is something you have practiced and can tap into and apply to your life. This mental and physical process of winning is ingrained in you as a seasoned athlete. Your specialized body and mind, my friend, are already built to win! Even though I haven't done a back handspring in a while, if I attempted one right now I would not have to start from scratch and relearn the skill from drills on the floor, my body has the memory of how to perform this skill (though as we age, we can't quite physically do what we use to). Your **past training experiences and successes are available for new challenges**; they are your proven track record, your springboard.

Through rigorous years of training you learned the elements of winning: how to be disciplined, committed, connected, powerful, goal oriented, focused, faithful, and so on. Do you know how invaluable that is . . . or better yet, how valuable you are?

For you, going for your goals may have occurred very naturally because you were actively pursuing your dreams and you were inspired. For instance, you didn't have to think about being committed, you did the work because you wanted to improve your game and would do whatever that required.

According to dictionary.com inspiration means:

1. To fill with enlivening or exalting emotion.
2. In spirit, breathing life into.[8]

We should be taught not to wait for inspiration to start a thing. Action always generates inspiration. Inspiration seldom generates action. – Frank Tibolt

Most likely you felt this inspiration in sport, and it came from action.

Are you ready to take action? _____

Are you ready to say YES to the game of life? _____

Just because you have retired from sport does not mean you have to sit on the bench for the rest of your life and think about the glory days. If you are ready to get back in the game

---

[8] www.Dictionary.com. Retrieved July, 2005.

of life, and be coached to a new way of thinking, using some trained behaviors, let this season of your life begin!

The following Five Secrets will set you up for a winning life beyond sport.

Secret 1: Identity
Secret 2: Vision
Secret 3: Foundation
Secret 4: Plan
Secret 5: Structure and Support

Because most athletes like to keep score, I've developed a questionnaire and point system that will track your progress as you work through this book. Here, you are only competing against you, striving to be your best. *Go for gold!*

Insights:

_____

_____

_____

_____

_____

_____

_____

_____

_____

_____

_____

_____

_____

Chapter Three

Beginning Assessment

1. How inspired are you currently about your life beyond sport? (0 is not at all, 10 is absolute inspiration)

_____

_____

_____

_____

2. Rate your ability to exist in this world without your sport defining you. (0 is I am completely defined by my sport, 10 is my relationship to my sport is healthy)

_____

_____

_____

_____

3. How confident are you in your ability to win in life overall beyond sport? For example: financially, relationally, emotionally, physically, and professionally? (0 is not confident at all, 10 is extremely confident)

_____

_____

_____

_____

4. Do you have a clear direction and plan for your life beyond sport? (0 is I feel completely lost, 10 is I feel completely clear)

_____

_____

_____

_____

5. List three results you would like to accomplish in your life now.

_____

_____

_____

_____

_____

_____

6. What is the #1 thing that stops you from achieving those results currently?

_____

_____

_____

_____

7. What are your top three challenges in facing the transition beyond sport?

_____

_____

_____

_____

_____

_____

_____

_____

_____

_____

_____

8. What do you still want to do while you're here on earth?

_____

_____

_____

_____

_____

_____

_____

_____

_____

_____

_____

_____

_____

_____

_____

_____

_____

_____

_____

9. What's one thing you want to get out of this workbook?

_____

_____

_____

_____

_____

_____

_____

_____

_____

_____

_____

_____

Share Opp- @transitionwhatnow post the one thing you want to get out of this workbook and #gameoflife.

The goal of the assessment is to assess where you are now, gain awareness, and compare to the End Assessment.

Assessment Insights:

_____

_____

_____

_____

_____

_____

_____

_____

_____

_____

_____

_____

Chapter Four

Secret 1: Identity

What many athletes reported they had lost in retirement from sport was a mastery over their lives because they no longer felt as confident in their ability as a retired athlete to achieve the kinds of success in non-sport areas or even to live a satisfactory life after sport. – Scott Tinley

One of the biggest challenges athletes face in retirement is with identity. Many athletes say:

- I define myself with my sport.
- Sport was not what I did but who I was.
- They treated me like who I was, a pro athlete.[9]

Can you relate to being identified by your sport?

I was team captain of the Penn State University women's gymnastics team. It was my senior year, and this was our year to win big! Our senior class was among the best leaders Penn State has ever seen. We were talented, strong, hungry, united, and full of leadership. On January 16, the second home meet of the season, I blacked out on my bar dismount (two flips, one twist), landed- discombobulated, with one leg behind me- on my back, and brought the packed crowd to a silence. Although my leg was in two places, I was calm. My orthopedist rushing to the scene, snapped my leg back in place and carried me off the floor to assess the injury. His

---

[9] Baillie, P. H. F., & Danish, S. J. Understanding the career transition of athletes. Sport Psychologist, 1992. p77-98.

hands were on my leg, and his head slowly bowed in regret. My heart beat heavily. After a few seconds, he raised his head and looked into my eyes. He spoke the three dreaded letters no athlete ever wants to hear . . . "You tore your A -C -L" [And much more]. I lost it! One minute all of my goals and aspirations were possible, and the next minute, as I collapsed to the floor, so too did my dreams. I was absolutely devastated. My senior season was over. I was no longer a gymnast. I wept.

For my whole life, I was "Janae the gymnast." It even sounded cute, a little ring to it if you will. I walked like a gymnast, I talked like a gymnast, I moved about the world like a gymnast, and at 4'11", I embodied gymnast. All of my life I was introduced as "the gymnast." When people talked to me they wanted to know about gymnastics. **My identity was wrapped up in my sport.**

Researchers Baillie & Danish found that sport defines our self-image. From a young age, accomplished athletes "receive preferential treatment for their talent and potential improvement."[10]   As suggested by Heyman and Andersen, "Young athletes obtain a foreclosed identity when they identify exclusively with the role of athlete."[11]

"Oops!" I would say I obtained a foreclosed identity. I identified pretty much exclusively with the role of an athlete. As you may know, gymnasts have a bit of a reputation for being sheltered. I was probably one of the least sheltered accomplished gymnasts I knew. Yet, I still managed a

[10] Baillie, P. H. F., & Danish, S. J. Understanding the career transition of athletes. Sport Psychologist, 1992. p77-98.
[11] Hayman and Andersen. Journal Of Excellence. Issue #13. 2009 (McKnight et al). p 63.

foreclosed identity, and I lost a lot of confidence along with losing my sport. The identity piece is hard to escape as a high level athlete. The bottom line is that you are more than just your sport.

I will say this again because it is really important: **You are more than just your sport.** You are not what you do. The essence or core of you is who you are in the world. You are here for a purpose. Don't buy into the temptation of success. We know it, we love it, we become blindly addicted to the praise, accolades, and special treatment. We think we will be fulfilled with the splendor, the glitter.

Don't buy into the empty promises. I recently watched a documentary called *I AM*[12], which is about a famous Hollywood producer. Tom Shadyac earned all the success he dreamed of. He owned elaborate estates in Italy, Monaco, Mexico, and Beverly Hills. When the movers finished moving the last piece of furniture into his newest 7,000 square foot [un]humble abode, he stood in his foyer completely stunned and saddened. He was stunned by feelings of emptiness. He did not feel more fulfilled...rather...more empty than before. However, it took a very serious cycling accident for him to have his spiritual awakening thought of, "What is this all for?" An awakening to the temptation of success. Do not buy into the shiny bling, accolades and need to feel special amongst fellow mankind.

A normal everyday person had a different angle on being identified by what we do or have. I had a life coaching client that was working on a relationship goal. She quit her

---

[12] "I AM – The shift is about to hit the fan." www.Iamthedoc.com. Dir. Tom Shadyac. Flying Eye Productions. 2010

full-time job (that she was unhappy with) and decided to wait tables until she figured out what she wanted. She once said to me, "Why would a man even like me? I don't have anything to offer him; I live with my parents and I don't have a career."

Wrong! What you have to offer a man/woman is not what you do or what you have accomplished, but who you are and who you are shaped to be- your gifts, heart, abilities, personality, experiences.[13]

What you have to offer the world is not your identity as a basketball, soccer, or hockey player, but the many unique traits that make you who you are. I had this confused for a long time. I questioned: if I am not a gymnast then who am I?

When working on the mental game with my clients, who are current athletes, I help them define a mental state ideal for training and competition. This is a very powerful way for athletes to get in the zone and rock their game. I am no longer competing, however I realized it is equally powerful to define who I want to be in life—as a wife, mother, business owner, leader, friend, etc. This helps set the tone of my home and life. I call this mindset tool my **"PIC"-Personal Identity Characteristics.** I strive to be in my PIC (bold, fun, relish) throughout my day. When I am not (which can be often) I stop and breathe in my words. I just think "lighten up and relish in the fleeting moments" and it really helps. My family likes that commitment, too! My PIC has changed throughout the years, as my life has changed. I

---

[13] Rees, Erik. S.H.A.P.E. - Finding and Fulfilling Your Unique Purpose in Life. Grand Rapids: Zondervan, 2008.

chose "bold" because it has paved the way for me and helps me powerfully act instead of caring what others think. I chose "fun" because I am naturally a fun person, but at times I can get caught up in being "serious mom who has to get stuff done." Lastly, I chose "relish" because of the movie suggestion below. With my current lifestyle it is easy to get caught up in busyness and insignificant things rather than focusing on what is pleasant in each moment.

Now it's time to create your own Personal Identity Characteristics. Choose three words that define who you are committed to being. Who are you when you are at your best? What character traits of yours are needed or do you want to be known for? Here is an idea bank to choose from, but feel free to think of your own: *leader, fun, loving, strength, power, joy, honest, faithful, focused, trustworthy, motivating, inspiring, servant, generous, compassion, integrity, humble, creative, happy, bold, wise, humorous, courageous, calm, cheery, simple, confident, responsible, dauntless, kind, adventurous, free, capable, balanced, noble, optimistic, satisfied, respectful, charismatic, organized, hardworking, helpful, warrior, imaginative, loyal.*

- **Step 1: Choose 3 words that represent your new "identity."**
  1._____
  2._____
  3._____

- **Step 2: Write your three words on a sticky note:**
  "I am_____
  _____ "

- Step 3: Post your new "identity" on your bathroom mirror, cell phone wallpaper, somewhere you will see it.

Share Opp- @transitionwhatnow post your new "identity" and #MyID.

Read it daily, let it sink in. Bring your "identity" into all areas of your life. Start being those three things to yourself, to friends, to loved ones, at work, etc. When you are not being those words, notice and do one thing to shift into your "identity."

- ★ Give yourself 2 points for completing all 3 steps of the exercise: _____

   Movie to watch:

- ★ *About Time* (2013)- Pay close attention to the 2nd and 3rd secret to happiness and the word **RELISH**!

- ★ Give yourself 1 point if you watched the movie._____

- ★ Give yourself 2 points if you have redefined your "identity"and realize you are more than your sport._____

Note: Included in this workbook are exclusive celebrity and college athlete interviews. The celebrity interviews are audio transcribed, abbreviated versions.

Celebrity Interview: Mary Lou Retton

Janae- *I would like to introduce one of the most popular athletes in the world! She captured the heart of America in the 1984 Olympic Games with two perfect 10.0 routines to win the first ever All-Around gymnastics gold medal for USA. As one of the top 10 most admired public figures she has a 12 year list of awards and accomplishments that are way too many to rattle off. I will include some highlights: 3 Hall of Fame inductees, Sports Illustrated Sportswoman of the Year, The Mary Lou Retton award and let us not forget a loving husband and four amazing daughters (which I am sure is one of the biggest accomplishments). I just want to say we are honored today to be with you thank you very much for giving us the gift of your time.*

Mary Lou- *Well thank you so much! Gymnastics has given, and my accomplishments, have given so much to me so if I can help in any way to give back to those future athletes I would be more than happy. So thank you.*

Janae- *As one of America's most admired athletes who absolutely reached the top of your game... was there one moment you can remember when you decided you weren't going to be a gymnast anymore? And how did you make that decision?*

Mary Lou- *There absolutely was a defining moment. I knew in 1984 Los Angeles Olympic Games would be my only shot. You as a gymnast, know it is very rare as a gymnast- although it's a little more time these days because you can make somewhat more of a career out of it actually physically doing this sport... but it is a relatively short career. And I knew that '84 Los Angeles was my shot!!! I would be 16, I would be prime. I knew I would not do college gymnastics. When the Olympics were over at 16, I continued competing at a pretty high level competitively competing until I was 18. I retired from competitive gymnastics and went to college as a normal student. It was after winning my third consecutive American Cup which is a pretty prestigious title in gymnastics. I knew that I wanted to finish on a high note I knew that that was it and it was time. I was 18.*

Janae- Like every athlete will sometimes face you had to make that transition from gymnast to life beyond sport. Think yourself back to that moment, what was the transition out of gymnastics like for you? What happened?

Mary Lou- It was very difficult. Most of us gymnasts at that high-level when you are competing World Championship, Olympic, Elite levels, you are in the gym 8 hours a day and are usually homeschooled. You have very few socialization skills...kindly and politically correct, what I mean is you are barefoot in a leotard your whole life. Then you're let out into the world and I was let out into a college environment. And my college years were not good ones. I faced jealousy, I faced young women, young girls being jealous and envious of me. And here I was the sweet little Mary Lou, I haven't changed any. In fact one of my friends you might know the name; Michael Jordan, he is a friend of mine. He said to me (right after the Olympics I had the opportunity to sit down with him) "Fame does not change you, it changes everyone around you." It doesn't -it changes everybody around you. I was still the same Mary Lou- that same Mary Lou that busted my rear 8 hours in the gym everyday, I had to sacrifice living away from home. People didn't like me for that. Of course as I look back now as a grown adult, I was a young childish 18 year old in college. But it was very difficult. I didn't have socialization skills most of my friends were my teammates, in the same situation as myself. It was the small fraternity or sorority of people who you didn't have to explain things to- you just got it. If you are feeling down, you are emotionally drained or you are physically exhausted you didn't have to say it you didn't have to explain yourself your friends- your teammates got it. So my communication skills were not very good when I entered into the real world. Also the biggest obstacle I personally had to overcome was in decision making. My whole life since I was 7 years old I've been coached. This is what you wear... was it good enough? My whole life was like this. So when I entered into the real world at 18 I was looking back behind for my coaches, "Did I do it right?" "Was this what I was supposed to do?" That was the hardest thing for me to do, this decision making without that coach giving me the high five, "Hey that's good!"

Janae- That is perfect and right on! I would say that as a college gymnast at my level as well that was huge for me. My self expression or ability to actually have discipline without being told what to do when and where and why and how? All you had to do is show up.

Janae- Clearly when you were leaving gymnastics I see you as somebody who exemplifies "sweet Mary Lou" like you said. Just that incredible smile that you always wear and you have continued to impact America and be an ambassador for our sport beyond your transition. In your transition just focusing on the success, I feel like you did really well and were successful with the transition.

Mary Lou- Hmmm. What you see is what you get with me. I do not see myself as anything special. I see my teammates who put in the hours and the years and the work just like I did. I happened to win I happen to be on that night. I happened to have the good Lord bring that coach into my life that brought out that talent that He had given me. We all have a gift, mine just happened to be athletics. We have to find that gift. I feel so fortunate and so blessed, Janae, that I was able to do that. It just happened to be watched by the world. Which is why I am what you call "famous." I hate that word but people use it, especially in today's day and age. I think that my biggest accomplishment in transitioning is when I made that jump from an athlete –actually being in a leotard in the gym to speaking (and I've been doing motivational talks now for 20 years) so I think my reputation and my story has a life of its own because there's been so many gold medalist since me and so many speakers since me and I still continue to work so that makes me feel good. That means, "Hey I have a great story to tell." When people see an athlete especially in a situation like myself, you know, the Olympic games standing on the award stand/ platform- national anthem playing –flag is rising- gold medal around your neck –singing... it's the epitome, the pinnacle of athletics. People just think "Oh wow! How great!" And it is! It is indescribable. You can't describe those words or feeling. But [they] don't get the story of adversity and the struggle and obstacles you have to overcome to get to that point. To me I have my story and I share it so to make that jump from physical athlete to speaker for 20 years is a big accomplishment and something I'm very proud of. And it wasn't easy to do. It wasn't easy to do. I think I have a good personality that is very conducive to that business.

Janae -Yes. You are a true ambassador for gymnastics! What would you say was the most challenging aspect of retirement?

Mary Lou- Probably the physical part of it. Putting on weight. Of course going from the gym 8 hours a day from a pretty strict regimen– you go to college and you're eating pizza at 2 o'clock in the morning. I've never done that before in my life!!! ... It was fun and it was great and you look up in a couple of months and I put on some weight; which was completely normal as I was starting to finally develop and mature into a young woman. So all of that combined– that was the most challenging and difficult part for me. All gymnasts go through that. I don't know about other sports, but I know gymnasts do. I spent a good 3 years a little embarrassed by my body because I had put on weight. And I am 4'9" so you know the struggle of putting on 5 pounds, 10 pounds is a lot. And having people stare at me "Ohhh that's Mary Lou" and "eeww" and all the comments you pretend not to hear but you really do. It wasn't because you had a coach telling you, "you need to lose weight" or a judge saying "hey you could drop a few" or you feeling self conscious because you're practically naked in a leotard– it's something that you come to terms with and say "Hey I want to do this for me. I want to be healthy, I want to start exercising." Not in a gymnastics gym but in a regular gym I started exercising and felt great! Well, it took a few years to reach that point and that contentment, for me.

Janae– What would have been helpful for you in transition? Something that you didn't have that you could see looking back that would've been helpful?

Mary Lou– A mentor who had been through it. A coach just like you and I are talking about somebody that really... that would have, you know, I had to go through that whole struggle of decision making and learn about failures. I had to learn that has a young adult. But just to be able to speak to somebody and talk to somebody. And cry and share my frustration with. I was really the first. I come from a family from small town America, wonderful parents but not much help in that thing. I just really *felt like I was on my own. I would've felt quite a load off to have a mentor, would have been a huuuuge help. A HUGE help.*

Janae– What advice do you, Mary Lou, have for athletes today who are facing the challenge of leaving their sport?

Mary Lou– Well, I think it is always better to leave your sport on your own terms. You leave when you want to. Leave with a good taste in your mouth. My advice is to not try to be superwoman/man. Try not to leave the sport and enter into a somewhat normal life without asking for help. How would you do that? Talk to people. Brainstorm with people. If I had a group or mentor it would have just made it all so much more enjoyable for me. That is the advice I would say is to have that team of...not coaches intimate in the sense that we grew up with, but have that other team of help set up for you. It will help tremendously. The antidote to lifelong friends.

Janae– Have you seen what might be the switch for some athletes who can't give up that limelight and then something clicks and they shift into acceptance and moving forward?

Mary Lou– You know it might be age. It might be physical. In my mind I might think I can get out there and do some stuff but if you get out there, it's very humbling. These younger kids come over and just whip you. It may be an age and just physical limitation at that point. You were in your prime– you retire– you miss it– you try and come back...Mark Spitz tried to do it and physically you just can't keep up. Your body is past, just like giving birth; God has a specific time frame for when a woman can give birth and when she passes that age complications can come into play. I think the same as true in athletics. Especially in our sport. It's such a short career. You peak at such a young age.

The older you get –the more mature you get– the more body you have the harder a sport is to do. I think just age and just physical limitations can sometimes determine that for that athlete.

Janae– One of the areas I work with my athletes– in creating a life beyond sport that can exceed the rewards and glory of being an athlete. Clearly there are many. And many athletes that I speak to live their life constantly looking back, looking in rearview mirror, at the point in their life they peaked in sport. They cannot even see the possibility of creating a life better than that feeling. So what would you recommend for these athletes who cannot see the possibility of an even more rewarding life beyond sport?

Mary Lou– Oh just keep trudging on because the best is yet to come. Oh my goodness. It is easy for someone to say this word, it's hard to live it. But I am living my dream. I am really living my dream right now. Married 16 years, mother of four beautiful children. I did something when I was 16 that was pretty phenomenal. I won the Olympics wheeeew! That's pretty big but I'm doing exactly, living exactly where I want to be right now. Life is so good. Life is hard and life is so good. Just keep trudging along because it's just beginning. This is just beginning and you will go through so many different stages in your life. One may be better, one may be worse. But they are all good, and they all learning experiences.

Janae– Thank you so much for your words, for you time. You are an inspiration to the world and I am honored to have this time with you to spread your cheer and wisdom.

Mary Lou– You are sooo welcome!! This was fun and it is great to share. You are doing such needed work. There are so many out there that would benefit from your work. I wish I had it. Thank you Janae!

Interview Takeaway:

_____
_____
_____
_____
_____
_____
_____
_____
_____
_____

College Interview: Tom

(Former Penn State University Men's Hockey, current Medical Sales Rep.)

Janae– What has worked about transitioning out of sport for you and the life you live today?

Tom– Sport has opened every door for me in my life, my family plays sports (hockey) my best friends are athletes.

Janae– What doesn't work about your life after sport? What's missing?

Tom– I still enjoy playing hockey, basketball, golf, surfing, snowboarding, but I miss playing at the national level.

Janae- Have you discovered a new dream that has you jumping out of bed each morning? Or are you surviving?

Tom- *I use what I have learned in college hockey and apply it to work on a daily basis. I like competition on the ice and in the workplace.*

Janae- What dreams do you have on life support? What visions have you not yet given life to because it is not the right time, or too scary, or just a dream, or not enough money/time, or?

Tom- *The hardest thing is realizing that there is life after college and like I said above I still enjoy coaching and playing hockey on a regular basis. I think that most athletes get bitter because they don't compete anymore. I often think about influential coaches in my life and I try to give back to the sport. Most athletes fear coaching and simply walk away... I would suggest coaching at some point after playing a sport it gives me so much satisfaction to see youngsters achieving their goals. So to answer the question above- I dream that some hockey player looks back on their sports career and says "Coach Tom was a big part of my success."*

FOLLOW UP:

Janae- Here we are nearly 10 years later. What have you accomplished in this time?

Tom- *I work for Valeant Labs as a Device Rep and I was the assistant coach for the NJ Outlaws Minor Pro hockey team that won the FHL Single A Pro Championships in 2012.*

Janae– How has your experience as an athlete propelled your future?

Tom– Work Hard– Play Hard the Penn State Way! Also to deal with adversity – also the Penn State (athlete) Way.

Janae– What was the most challenging point of your life post retirement from sport?

Tom– Not playing and becoming a coach, it's harder to teach!

Janae– For me, the challenges in transition from sport diminished when I became less and less able physically to compete at a high level, having a family and finding my purpose spiritually. What was that point of acceptance and moving forward for you?

Tom– Same.

Janae– What is your advice for athletes transitioning out of sport today who are not yet at the stage of acceptance?

Tom– Change your game to play with less stress on your body, learn the business side of your sport and also attempt coaching – you will appreciate your sport more!

Janae– Thank you!

Interview Takeaway:

_____

_____

_____

_____

_____

_____

_____

_____

_____

_____

Insights:

_____

_____

_____

_____

_____

_____

_____

_____

_____

_____

_____

_____

_____

_____

_____

_____

_____

_____

_____

_____

_____

Chapter Five

Secret 2: Vision

Begin with the end in mind. – Stephen R. Covey

There was a "famous study" done in the 1950's on a Harvard University graduating class. According to researchers, only 3 percent of the graduates had clearly written goals. Twenty years later they polled as many members of that same graduating class as they could and found that the 3 percent who had written down their goals had accumulated more wealth than the other 97 percent combined!

This study has been published in more than twenty books. The catch is, however, that no one can verify that the study ever took place. It sounds great, but as far as my research carried me, verification cannot be found. I want this study to be true, it is very compelling. However, a new study was done due to the popularity of the Harvard goals study.[14] And of course it did in fact reveal the positive effect of written down goals. The study proves there is no match for a motivated person with clearly written goals and accountability.

Can you imagine approaching a season or competition with the attitude, "Ahhh, we'll see what happens, no need for a goal, we're talented."? No, you had clear goals.

I worked with a Division 1 NCAA gymnastics team that had

---

[14] Matthews, Gail, Ph.D., Dominican University. Gail Matthews Written Goal Study Dominican University. Retrieved February 12, 2014.

only been in existence for four years. Like any new sports program, they were expected to take a number of years to earn a reputation, and needed solid recruits to slowly build their program and results.

The team's coaches, however, chose to blow logic out of the water; they set a goal to make it to NCAA National Championships by their fourth year in existence. This was unheard of. Many laughed. Many doubted this lofty goal, but that didn't matter to this team. They had the vision, the game plan, and most importantly the belief that they could do it.

And they did it! They beat a team that had won four out of the previous six National Championships. This gigantic win granted them their goal—to compete in the NCAA National Championships, placing in the top twelve collegiate gymnastic teams in the nation. Against many odds, they overcame . . . and it all started with one simple goal.

Now that you grasp the power of your goals and intentions, even beyond sport, let's design some for your life. What are your dreams, goals, and aspirations? If you knew you couldn't fail, what would you take on? What are the dreams you had when you were young? What do you feel like you are designed to do? What impact or legacy do you want to leave in this life? What are your secret passions? What makes you mad, sad, or glad that you want to work on? I want you to think so big for your life that it scares and excites you. Typically, especially if you have already achieved a high level of personal success, fulfillment comes from serving others. You do not have to focus there, but it is an area to ponder.

Exercise:

- **Step 1: Create your Personal Vision List (PVL)**

  Below, write a list of all the things you want in life (material and nonmaterial). Be specific. State your goals in the positive, not the negative. For instance, you could have a goal to stop thinking negatively, but if you are not thinking negatively what are you doing? Yes, thinking positively. Instead of "don't think as negatively," simply write, "think more positively."

  Also note where the focus is. This point is very important. I have seen athletes write goals like, "To be pain free." Do you see the pitfall with that? The focus is on the pain. What works better is, "To have a perfectly functioning and healthy body." Same thing with the goal, "To get out of debt." Where is the focus? You got it—on debt! A more powerful version may be, "To have $1,000 in savings by November 1."

  Think both short and long-term here. Choose statements that fire you up when you read them. You may put your items in list form or paragraph form; it's your choice. You may want to refer to your answers from the "Beginning Assessment" in chapter three, as the answers may overlap.

My Personal Vision List:

_____

_____

_____

_____

- **Step 2: Double check the list**

   Do these items fire you up, light you up, make your heart beat, and call you forward into action? If not, refine them.

Share Opp- @transitionwhatnow post one aspect of your vision you are excited about and #goingforit.

- **Step 3: Read your list daily for at least 30 days**

   Put your list in your wallet, cell phone, tablet, computer, planner, or on your bathroom mirror, desk or bedside table—somewhere you will be forced to read it every day. Ideally, read the list out loud at least once every day. Picture yourself achieving and becoming your vision. Soon you may not need the list because you will know it by heart. You will begin to produce the results you want. Do not fret about the how right now. Practice trusting the unseen. By setting your intentions and being committed to them, ideas will come, opportunities will present themselves, implementation steps will come in Secret 4.

Have you ever read *The Hobbit*, or seen the movie? You will see this concept quite profoundly! Although it is fiction, I took notice of little Frodo setting his mind to the various daunting battles; although he did not know all of the "hows," he stepped up to the plate, and just when the situation looked dim, the right tool, thought, person, or creature, etc. would present itself. The how took care of itself in the heat of the moment. This is not too far off from real life. Just when you think you cannot go any further, something happens that allows you to press on. Trust life.

- ★ Give yourself 2 points if you completed all 3 steps of your Personal Vision List _____

  Movie(s) to watch:

- ★ *Prefontaine* (1997), *Without Limits* (1998) or *Home Run* (2013)

- ★ Give yourself 1 point for the movie you watched _____

- ★ Give yourself 2 points if you have created a new vision for your life that you are inspired about _____

Celebrity Interview: Joe Ehrmann

Janae– Here with us today we have Joe Ehrmann. Joe was a professional football player for 13 years. He was the Colts Man of the Year, Syracuse's most distinguished alumni award recipient, He was featured on the cover of Parade magazine for 'The most important coach of America,' also the subject of New York Times bestseller– "Season of Life," the co-founder of Door, and Baltimore's Ronald McDonald House. He is now a high school coach, seminar leader and highly sought after speaker. We are very thankful to have you with us today Joe. To start off, I would like to have you briefly explain to the listeners a bit about the driving force behind your life's work that has led to such accolades.

Joe– Well it is great to be with you Janae. I am someone who grew up right at the convergence of the Civil Rights movement, the war on poverty, the women's rights movement, and the anti war movement. I think that was the right time of asking all the right questions of value and worth in human beings. Apart from race and gender it was about opportunity and equality. Those things marked me. Those questions and that era marked me for a lifetime. For the last 40 years or so I have been working on those issues in one form or another. Both in the church and on the street and in the world of sports.

Janae– That is great. My husband has been listening to the biography of Martin Luther King and we both have been extremely inspired by all that we hear. I cannot imagine what it was like to live around that time period.

Joe– Well Dr. King was a great mentor of mine. And I'm very fortunate that the definitive historian of Martin Luther King, Taylor Branch, just wrote a 3 volume series on Dr. King's life, is also a friend of mine. Dr. King asked a question that has really marked and shaped my thoughts, "Life's most persistent and urgent question is what are you doing for others?" He certainly was the embodiment of an others centered and others focused person of this world.

Janae– I am 30 years old and I feel like it's taken me this long to get that. But I've seen a transition in my life, which will talk about a little bit later, where as a star athlete I think your life at times, can be so much about yourself and that pursuit of your athletic career. Granted it is a great vehicle you can use 'for others.' But with many athletes, I feel, it becomes a selfish pursuit. Upon retirement that is the challenge for some athletes; that transition from self to others. It's much more rewarding. Again it has taken me to this point to really comprehend that my life is not about me; it's about serving others. With that being *said, you obviously have been very successful both on and off the field. I think I know the answer to this but I would like you to answer the question; What has been more fulfilling to you- playing in the NFL or the work you do now in life, and why?*

Joe- Clearly, the work that I am doing now has much more impact. It transcends my own personal goals, wants and ambitions which was the primary focus when I was an athlete. It's really paradoxical because if you think of athletics today, talking of the world of team sports. Team sports are all about two things; they're all dependent upon the forming of relationship in sports. They call that chemistry. We call it being in the flow or the zone. Team sports are dependent upon people learning how to relate, connect, trust and to depend on each other.

The second thing team sports are all about is having a commitment that you submit your own personal goals and ambitions for the greater cause of the team. You have all of these athletes working in an environment where the very foundation is about relationships and yet it's so individualistic. I think part of that is because that's how we are, specifically boys, in this country; that is how we are raised. Boys are taught to be autonomous. To be independent. You're supposed to be your own man. Our paradigm for masculinity is about comparing our gifts, abilities, possessions, and comparing that with someone else. And then competing for some corresponding social value there. So it takes a certain amount of maturity. As part of the corrective, we need to bring into sports; rather than a 'win at all costs,' and individual goals and attainment; How do you teach kids to be team players that are focused on relationship with her teammates and submit their own personal goals towards the greater common goal of the entire team?

Janae– Would you mind taking us through the process of your retirement until now and some of the significant transitions you went through? Or events that have been the driving force in your life?

Joe– Well right in the middle of my career, I watched my little brother die of cancer. I spent 5 months in a pediatric oncology floor, with all of these other families that had children facing some kind of life threatening illness. In that waiting room I saw this incredible community. If you ever want to know where wisdom and truth is... it is in those waiting rooms because there you get a perspective about what is really important and what is really unimportant. And you had all of these families who have put their lives on hold– their vocational lives, their marriages, all of the responsibilities to support this child. And there is tremendous stress and duress.

After my brother's death, I began to re-evaluate my own life. I ended up working on creating a Ronald McDonald House here in Baltimore that has served over 35,000 families and helped support families in times of their greatest needs. I saw that I had this platform as an athlete. I went to Seminary, the last five years that I played. I had a spiritual awakening. I started working in inner city Baltimore, working on real real tough communities. Working on issues of poverty, of racism, addictions and domestic violence, child sexual abuse and a host of issues. I then saw that perhaps the greatest crisis that (if you're going to deal with those issues there is even a bigger problem that needs to be addressed), to me the greatest crisis in America is the crisis of masculinity. The crisis about– what does it mean to be a man? How do boys know when they become men? Right behind that crisis is a growing crisis of femininity. How does a woman know when she becomes a woman? What are virtues and values of being a woman? I started looking at those issues for a long time. Then it became very clear to me that perhaps the greatest venue in America or platform to deal with America's deepest social problems is through sports. Sports engages more individuals, more families, more communities than any other cultural activity or institution or religion in America. It is in fact the secular religion of America. The high priest and pastor of that secular religion is the coach. That coach has tremendous power to be able to mark a young person's life for a lifetime. The question is; whether the coach uses that platform and power to positively impact young people holistically in every aspect of their lives or do they use the power to just kind of hurt and diminish them based on performance or status or some kind of ranking?

Janae- You are a catalyst to change our world! Athletes that are currently going through retirement may struggle with things like finances, relationships, addictions (gambling, sex, substance abuse, etc.). Sometimes they struggle with things like self identity and purpose. What was your experience with this and what is your advice to athletes facing challenges in transition today?

Joe- Well, I think again you have to do your own internal journey and understand false messaging. The problem is that sports are so elevated in our culture and within our communities and our families, that sometimes even parents and people that love that player; they identify more with that athlete's jersey than with that person. They buy into all these stereotypes. It leaves an athlete with a real identity crisis because once that jersey gets taken away (and everybody has to eventually give up their jersey and that spot on a team) then there's a real crisis about *Who am I? ...Who am I? What is my identity? What are my values and worth?*

What is inherent, that athletes while they're in the game, they have to maintain some kind of relationship some kind of authentic community where they are known for who they really are. And valued, accepted and appreciated for that. When athletes get out of the game and they don't have a sense of identity, boy they have to really do the internal work. They need to get with people that can help them process through that experience. And bring about the healing and wholeness there.

Janae – I have friends in Player Development (NFL) and they are smart, aware and able to help.

Joe– The question is getting the players to initiate and actually take advantage of them. But when I played until today, there is a whole resource a whole menu there for athletes to use. Those players that have a sense of vision about where they are going and have maintained some sense of values they utilize the resources. And you know by enlarge the NFL is composed of mostly terrific young men that have a great sense of social responsibility. Part of the problem is that the media continues to want to represent and portray some kind of rogue athletic or racial stereotype. That one guy who goes bad and that is the news story for a whole season as opposed to all of the guys that are using their platform, their resources, and their access to make their communities in this country much better. I think a big part of the problem is maybe representation of this.

Janae– How have you seen your beliefs impact your life and career?

Joe– Well my faith is kind of my driving force with all of my events and in my personal understanding. It is the essence of who I am. With all of this messaging taking place in the world the question is how do you reprogram that with some values-based kind of approach? For me personally, I am a man that does a lot of contemplation, and silence, and an awful lot of reflection and reflective writing. I'm just another struggling brother but everyday I try to get up and overcome my own... my own negative self concepts, doubts and misplaced values. You take it kind of day by day but my faith has been the platform and the sounding board for all of that.

Janae– Is there anything else you would like to add before we close just to encourage or challenge the athletes?

Joe– I would just encourage all athletes if I was going to recommend for them to do one thing I would recommend that they get a journal and have one place where they can go and write to an audience of one– yourself! And start doing your own reflective work about your own goals, visions and how you are feeling. All lasting and meaningful change starts on the inside and works its way out. We have to understand what's going on inside and writing that is just incredibly therapeutic and helpful.

Janae– Great. Thank you very, very much Joe... for your time and for all of your wisdom and insight. It is really incredible.

Joe– Well thank you! I'm just another struggling brother but we are all in this journey together. And just to close, Dr. King said "Life's most persistent and urgent question is; What are you doing for others?" So, thank you very much!

Interview Takeaway:

_____
_____
_____
_____
_____
_____
_____
_____
_____
_____
_____
_____
_____
_____
_____

College Interview: Carey

(Former elite and Penn State University Gymnast, former head gymnastics coach of The Ohio State University- current Associate Athletic Director, Wife, Mother):

Janae- What has worked about transitioning out of sport for you and the life you live today?

Carey- I transitioned out of my sport for a while and then ended up right back in the heart of it! Although I do not get to physically compete anymore, the day to day training, and the team atmosphere, as well as, the thrill of competition are still very real for me.

Janae– What doesn't work about your life after sport? What's missing?

Carey– I think the most difficult thing about life after sport is the loss of the close relationship with your teammates, and the proximity of the living situations, and being constantly surrounded by people who understand you and how you are feeling and what you are going through.

FOLLOW UP:

Janae– Here we are nearly 10 years later. What have you accomplished in this time?

Carey– Ten years later, the program has continued to improve and I am a much different coach than I was 10 years ago! So much has changed in recruiting, social media and connecting with kids today, I have really had to adjust my program to meet the changing needs of the athletes today.

In 2012 I was named the National Coach of the Year. That season, we finished 10th in the country, the best finish for Ohio State in over a quarter of a century. My graduation rate (APR) continues to be at 100% and for the past three years my team has held the highest team GPA at Ohio State out of all 36 Varsity sports (Team GPA 3.63).

Janae– How has your experience as an athlete propelled your future?

Carey– I often try to put myself in my athlete's shoes to get their perspective on various aspects of our program. Having been an athlete at PSU, there are many similarities to the cultures of competing in the Big Ten. There are also a lot of differences. Despite the differences, gymnastics has not changed all that much. "The hand goes down, and check me out!!" (Thank you Dr. Yukelson)...but that is sport. You train, you train, you prepare mentally and physically and then in that moment of truth you have to rise to the occasion, and that experience as an athlete time and time again has propelled me to be able to better prepare athletes for that moment in time.

Janae- What was the most challenging point of your life post retirement from sport?

Carey- I love competition, I thrive on it. When I was done competing, I felt like I didn't have a real purpose for working out...other than staying fit which is not that hard for me to do...so I turned to running and made training plan and ran races to get my competitive fix. I am not a very good runner, but having a plan and a deadline (race day!) helped me transition into life after sport.

Janae- What was that point of acceptance and moving forward for you?

Carey – Coaching for me has been that point of acceptance. Since I am around gymnastics all the time, and I know that I cannot physically do the sport any longer, it has been a smooth transition for me to be able to help other athletes be the best versions of themselves.

Janae- Research shows this transition is the most paralyzing for athletes who experience involuntary retirement. Which makes sense. I would also say that this challenge has a window of around 1 -10 years post retirement. What is your advice for *athletes transitioning out of sport today who are not yet at this stage of acceptance?*

Carey– My advice would be to find another talent they possess. For so many they have concentrated for so long on being an "athlete" that they might not even know what other talents they have! I would encourage them to do things that are uncomfortable for them, take an art or photography course...something that they have an interest in but have not been able to explore.

Interview Takeaway:

_____
_____
_____
_____
_____
_____
_____
_____
_____

Insights:

_____
_____
_____
_____
_____
_____
_____
_____

Chapter Six

Secret 3: Foundation

Your opponent, in the end, is never really the player on the other side of the net, or the swimmer in the next lane, or the team on the other side of the field, or even the bar you must high-jump. Your opponent is yourself, your negative internal voices, your level of determination. - Grace Lichtenstein

I am sure you all remember pre-season quite well, although maybe you called it something different. The concept is the same: During this time, you would build your foundation and prepare for game time. In sport training, you have to get stronger, faster, and higher. This is like the Olympic motto: Citius, Altius, Fortius (or, "Faster, Higher, Stronger"). Now it is time to work on skill, strengthening, resiliency, and making your foundation as flawless as possible. This will set the foundation for success in this season of life!

Exercise 1: Integrity is Key

In order for a building to stand, it must have strong integrity. Likewise, in order for you to perform, you must have strong integrity. What happens when the integrity of a building is compromised? It crumbles under pressure. You are not exempt.

Here is how Dictionary.com defines integrity:

1. Possession of firm principles—the quality of possessing and steadfastly adhering to high moral principles or professional standards
2. Completeness—the state of being complete or undivided
3. Wholeness—the state of being sound or undamaged[15]

What is encouraging is that you can control your integrity. You can build and maintain a solid structure. There are many things or thoughts we are tolerating in our life that drain energy and keep us from being sound/integral.

- **Step 1: Create your Personal Integrity List (PIL). Make a list of all the things that are incomplete or not in integrity with your life.**

  Your PIL is rightfully named. Someone who is defined as a "pill," is annoying and hard to swallow. So to is this list of items you have been avoiding. It is wildly energizing to begin tackling these items. What is still incomplete in your life? What is causing fatigue in your life? What have you said you were going to do and have not done, or what have you started and not finished? A large one may be with your athletic career. Is there something you did not achieve, something you missed out on, a goal you did not go for? When your career ended too early, was there some unfinished business? Other examples might include: a damaged relationship, dirty car, unorganized drawers, back taxes, car insurance at an old address, borrowed

[15] www.Dictionary.com. Retrieved July, 2005.

money, giving in to anger, forgetting to send a thank you card, not following through with your word, needing to paint the house, an unreturned call to a friend or a family member, clutter piles, a past-due doctor visit, and so on. Take note: This is not just a to-do list; these are personal integrity items—things you keep saying you want to do yet don't do.

The following are items I need to tackle on my Personal Integrity List (I left a lot of space because it is normal to have a lot of items):

_____

_____

_____

_____

_____

_____

_____

_____

_____

_____

_____

_____

_____

_____

_____

_____

_____

_____

_____

_____

_____

_____

_____

_____

_____

_____

_____

_____

_____

_____

_____

_____

_____

_____

_____

- **Step 2: Set a date**

  Put a date next to each item indicating when you will complete it. It may be something you physically have to do (I will hire help to organize my finances by day/month/year), an attitude you need to change (I will not yell, but speak lovingly to my wife at all times by day/month/year), a conversation you need to have (I will call Sam by day/month/year), an action you need to take (I will start my new business by day/month/year), a journaling exercise (I will write out my positive and negative consequences to this decision by day/month/year), or something you may need further support with. Stop avoiding or procrastinating—take action now.

- **Step 3: Put the PIL items in your calendar**

  Schedule it in! Not in pencil—that is easily erased by the many circumstances in life that come up. Obviously, you may use your calendar/planner of choice—paper, wall, phone, tablet, computer, etc. Practice putting your personal integrity list items first, followed by the daily circumstances or dramatics that seem to get in the way. Enjoy the difference.

Share Opp- @transitionwhatnow post one item you tackled on your PIL and # how you feel (#energized, #wildlyenergized, #walkingonsunshine, #free...).

  ★ Give yourself 2 points for setting up all 3 steps of the PIL _____

Exercise 2: Dump the 'Stinkin Thinkin'

If you recorded your every thought, what percentage do you think would be negative thoughts (or what is referred to as negative self talk)? I have heard that for the average person, 70 percent of our thoughts are negative. If that statistic is too high, let's say yours is 40 percent—that is still alarming!

Wherever a thought goes, a chemical goes with it. That is how the body works. For example, stress hormones go with fear thoughts. Adrenaline, Norepinephrine and Cortisol are three big stress hormones. These hormones are needed in certain cases (you have probably heard of the "fight or flight" mechanism of the sympathetic and parasympathetic nervous systems). However, our body is not meant to sustain the repetitive surge of stress hormones. Too much of these hormones will make your system crash. It can even cause your desired neural pathways, such as optimistic thoughts, to wither, which can lead to lasting impacts on your physical, mental, spiritual, and emotional well being.

"A massive body of research has now shown the mind-body connection is real- what we think affects us emotionally, intellectually and physically. For every thought that you meditate on, there is a physical reaction in the body in the form of electrical current traveling along the nerves in your brain and the production of various hormones and chemicals that flow throughout your entire body in response to those thoughts.

Our thoughts can absolutely dictate our future.

Here are some famous quotes concerning such thoughts:

Ralph Waldo Emerson: "You are what you think all day long."

J. Allen: "You are today where your thoughts have brought you. You will be tomorrow where your thoughts take you."

Dennis Watley: "It's not what you think that holds you back – it's what you think you are not."

Dr. Caroline Leaf: "As we think the brain has the ability to change itself for better or for worse. The recognition of this is a gigantic and significant leap in the history of mankind. It all starts and ends in the mind. Your mind is fully under your control. You can affect the whole way in which you function, just by controlling your thought life. When your thoughts are toxic, you are going to develop a dis-ease. Your thoughts have a direct link to your body through the mind body connection involving all the different nerve and chemical pathways via the hypothalamus."[16]

You may have heard of Epigenetics- where change exists in the gene function without change in the DNA sequence. Mind blowing! Thoughts are one way experts claim gene function change is possible. This can be bad. This can be very good! For now, it is another important reason to take charge of our thoughts.

I was working at Woodward sports camp. I was only there for one week with the kids. You cannot imagine the amount of negative self talk I heard: "I can't, I hate this, I will never be able to, I am not good at, I don't know how." The list was too long to mention. Another famous quote you may have heard from Henry Ford is, "Whether you think you can or you can't, either way you are right." Boy, was he on target! I found his quote to be true time and time again. Like a supernatural power, the gymnasts changed their thoughts, feelings, or words and, viola', their new attitude was met with success, or at least improvement!

Do you recall as an athlete how the little voice of negative self talk would overtake you? I do. It may have sounded different than above, but it definitely robbed you of confidence and success, and it likely still does.

Think about the bright side- with your current percentage of

[16] Strydom, MK. Healing Begins With Sanctification of the Heart. Harare, Zimbabwe. PrintWorks, 2013. 4th Edition. p 23

negative self talk, you have enjoyed the amount of success that you have. Can you imagine who you can be with even ten percent more positive, self-empowering thoughts? Do you think you might be a little less stressed, more balanced, more focused, more productive, more confident, more successful, with a healthier body, healthier relationships, etc.? I know you would! I have done negative self talk exercises with professional and Olympic athletes, we all have negative self talk that plays out on repeat. Let's tackle it.

Track your thoughts. Start noticing, observing and being conscious of all of the negative thoughts that you allow. You do not have to write them down, but pay attention to what goes on inside that mind of yours. By simply paying attention and observing your thoughts and noticing the negative self talk it will begin to disappear.

Be cautious of judging your negative thoughts and beating yourself up for having such thoughts. That is dumping more negative and feeding the cycle! One thing I tell clients, is to think about themselves at age six. You would not scold that child and say the nasty things you do to yourself now (e.g., "You are so stupid, you suck, what is wrong with you, you can't do it, you always make the wrong choice, you're not good at this"). Why do we say these things to ourselves now? It is harsh. It is toxic. Treat yourself now as you would your six year old self. You are still that worthy and vulnerable.

- **Step 1– Track your thoughts for three full days.**

  Wear a rubber band on your wrist, wear your watch on the opposite wrist or a penny in your shoe to remind you during the day and keep you on task. When you notice the rubber band, watch, or penny, take notice of your thoughts. Again, simply become aware of your negative thoughts and catch yourself thinking them. Just observe, and take mental notes. I am not asking you to be aware 24/7, but intermittently throughout the day. If you are ready for more you may snap your wrist (lightly) with the rubber band when you notice a negative thought. I did this exercise for a 3 day Elite training camp. We did a superhero theme and made superhero bracelets with our rubber bands. When they noticed their fear, doubt, intimidation, they would activate their superhero by snapping their bracelet and reading their superhero statements. What was fascinating was they were all so excited and all they did was notice and snap! No reading of the superhero statements needed. Just the snap seemed to do the trick. Sometimes it is the fun/humor that gets us out of our funk too. Yes I said funk. Get out of it.

★ **Give yourself 1 point for each full day you mentally tracked your thoughts (max 3)._____**

How will this help you dump your stinkin' thinkin'? Here is a notable example in my life:

My husband challenged me to stop speaking about death. I would constantly say, "That kills me." (about something that was funny), or, "You are so dead." (meaning, "I am going to get you."), or "I am dying of heat." You get the point. It is actually common language today.

At first when I was given the challenge, I didn't see what the big deal was. The more I thought about it, the more I understood the power of the spoken word and the impact on my life. Words send a message. For example, take the words: "I can" or "I can't." Both are used widely in athletics. Remember you are right either way.

I did not want to send the message of death to myself or anyone else. So I took on my husband's challenge. You cannot imagine how difficult this was! I almost gave up in the first two days. This may happen to you observing your negative thoughts.

Sometimes, I would say the word kill and not even realize it until my husband would point it out. Or I would say it and only notice it myself after it came out of my mouth, and get so frustrated because it seemed so uncontrollable. I wanted to win at this. First of all, I had nothing else to put in the place of kill/dead. I honestly thought I had taken on an impossible game. I saw no way to have choice with my words. It was so pitiful because it was just a word and yet I was so challenged.

Then one day I went to say something with "kill" in it and I completely stopped in my mouth tracks. I really caught myself! I used a replacement word/phrase such as; "I laughed so hard," and slowly but surely I have completely stopped. I may have said it one time in two months right after. Now, I cannot believe this was so difficult because I do not use these words anymore.

This isn't necessarily negative self-talk but it is an example of replacing what I say. By watching your self-talk you will certainly begin to choose what you say to yourself, and replace it with a more empowering word, phrase, or thought.

★ Give yourself 1 bonus point if you can notice your negative self talk and replace it with positive self talk._____ Bonus point.

We are way too powerful and valuable in this world to let negative thoughts control and dampen our lives and actions. Get serious about this. Notice the negative/disempowering thoughts and start choosing a more empowering version.

Movie(s) to Watch:

★ *Patch Adams* (1998)– How are you like Patch? Or how can you be more like Patch?

_____

_____

_____

(Watch either or both)

★ *Pollyanna* (1960)– How are you like Pollyanna? Or how can you be more like Pollyanna?

_____

_____

_____

★ Give yourself 1 point if you watched the movie._____

★ Give yourself 1 point if you have started building a solid foundation and you have noticed the impact on your life._____

Celebrity Interview: Dan Millman

Janae- *Welcome, Dan Millman. Dan is the author of 17 books, published in 29 languages. He's a former NCAA All-American who won several national titles and won the world trampoline championships. He was voted Senior Athlete of the Year at U.C. Berkeley, and later named to the U.C. Berkeley and USA Gymnastics Halls of fame. His most prominent book, Way of the Peaceful Warrior, was adapted to film in 2006, with Nick Nolte playing Dan's mentor, a service station mechanic he named 'Socrates'.*

Janae- *Dan, your time as a young athlete is known by millions of people because of your book and the movie. Would you share about your athletic career and how you dealt with retirement from competition?*

Dan- *Well, Janae, when my right leg was shattered in about 40 pieces just prior to my senior year at U.C. Berkeley, it seemed like an abrupt and involuntary retirement. My surgeon said I could probably walk normally again, but assumed my athletic career was finished. But, as I describe in Way of the Peaceful Warrior, I was able to recover and help my team win their first NCAA team championship.*

I can still recall that time. I was the last man up for our team in the final event — the horizontal bar. And we knew this: If I hit the best routine of my life, we might win. As I stood there, looking up at the bar, the past decade of my life and training flashed before me — and those grueling months to rehabilitate my leg — so with a focus and determination I had rarely experienced, I leaped up to the bar and began my routine. I pulled out all the stops, using an element I'd only accomplished a few times in practice — the coach, I learned later, gaped in shock when I did it. Then came the end of the routine and the all-important dismount. It came down to the dismount. I flew through the air, stretched for the ground, and stuck the landing. In that moment, I knew two things: First, before the judges even flashed their scores, I knew we had just won the NCAA Team Championships. Second, the moment I landed, I knew that I had retired from competition.

That summer, the Olympic coach called and encouraged me to try out for the 1968 team. But I needed to earn a living, so a return to competition wasn't feasible due to family circumstances — so I had the bittersweet experience of sitting in the stands at UCLA and watching one of my teammates earn a birth on the US Olympic Team.

During my years of training, my goals were short-term. I had vague ideas of what I wanted to do after retirement, but I didn't have any strategy. But my training had taught me some things about myself — for example, I enjoyed helping my teammates, and volunteered to teach young gymnasts at the local "Y." Self-knowledge may be one of the greatest potential gifts of sport. We can see our strengths and weaknesses, and how we deal with pressure.

I can still recall looking through the Classified Ads and then applying for a job selling life insurance, trying to find my way into the post-athletic world, leaving behind a decade-long habit of training every afternoon, enjoying the intensity and focus of competing. My new goal was earning a living in the real world. I discovered that I'd have to find out what I didn't want to do before I found what I really wanted to do. After graduation, I had no real back-up plan; I just let the currents of life take me. My life-insurance career lasted just a few months. It's a fine occupation for many people, but wasn't for me. I confronted the bigger questions, "What are my values? What are my talents? What are my interests?"

Then luck or destiny stepped in. I decided to drive back to Berkeley to visit my old coach, who told me that the Stanford University gymnastics coach position had just opened up. I made an appointment to speak with the athletic director the next day — and was appointed the head gymnastics coach.

I'm aware that many elite athletes who don't have clear aspirations outside of their sport, strive to stay connected to their area of expertise – to the memories and experiences they treasure. In my case, after four successful years as the Stanford coach, I ended up getting an offer to join the faculty of Oberlin College in Ohio, where I could teach innovative courses. By then, my interests had expanded out of the competitive arena, to training body, mind, and spirit. Around that time, I caught the writing bug. Many experiences followed. Eventually, with the success of my first book, my career and calling evolved into speaking as well as writing a series of books in the years to come.

Since relatively few athletes are able to (or even want to) stay in youthful athletic careers, which have an expiration date — and we need to pass the torch to a new generation of athletes. Some athletes attend professional school, or get trained in a trade, or go into real estate or other business ventures, applying the same focus and work habits that contributed to their athletic achievements.

Janae- Thank you for sharing that, Dan. Can you share some of the main qualities and lessons you learned from your years in sport that helped you later in life?

Dan- Sure. I view daily life as a form of spiritual weightlifting. If we don't lift weights we don't get stronger. All those years training, overcoming self-doubt and frustration, and learning persistence, taught me the value of adversity, of challenge. I view training in athletics as a form of voluntary adversity, leading to both strength and wisdom. One doesn't need to explain to an experienced athlete the value of patience and process, for example. That's why I tell athletes or people who are just training for exercise, "Don't dedicate your life to training; instead, dedicate your training to life."

In my own case, I discovered that there is a life after training — or rather, we continue training, but in a larger arena. We train to be better husbands or wives, better students and teachers. We train in a career. Of course all that is easy to say — still, as you can appreciate, we have to first go through a period of transition and transformation. It's not easy; it can be disorienting and discouraging. Only then do we draw upon the resources we developed in sport. Over time, we begin to see our time in sport as a metaphor for life. Sport teaches us about how reality works. We cannot pretend to be a gymnast or athlete in any other sport. We've learned that the rewards are in proportion to our preparation and effort. So even when we leave our sport, it doesn't leave us — all those years are not wasted, not thrown away. They carry us with momentum into a new arena called "daily life on Planet Earth."

Janae- Do you have any more advice or reminders, based on your own experience?

Dan– When my daughters were young, if they had asked me what sort of work they should do when they grew up, I would have said something like, "Find what you love and get someone to pay you for it." A bit idealistic but possible. Back in the late 1980s I heard a man named Ron Kaufman describe how he turned a love (and skill) throwing Frisbee flying disks into a profession as a Frisbee goodwill ambassador to a variety of different countries. Not everyone has this kind of luck — but most of us have heard the saying that "Luck happens when preparation meets opportunity." Once we get some clarity about our talents, values, and interests, and take stock of our preparation, the next step is to look for opportunities that may arise.

Janae– We've all seen retired athletes who feel so lost that they self-sabotage and self-medicate, abusing alcohol or other drugs — gambling and sex, that sort of thing. Do you think that coaching programs can help with that?

Dan– Some coaches might offer some tips or reminders, or at least provide access to career counselors and other resources to support athletes. Coaches can also serve as role models, and teach by their own example. The rare coach makes a point of meeting with each athlete, on occasion, and learning about their relationships and interests outside the sport, and whether they've given any thought to what they might like to do after they eventually retire. But I think the athletes and families and friends will bear the most responsibility for post-competition life.

Janae– Is there anything you might like to add?

Dan– It's difficult to see while we're immersed in the process of training, but sports are only a beginning, a preparation, not an end. Sport is a foundation for life, but not the whole of it. The larger arena awaits all of us. Eventually, we recognize that being an athlete is not who we are, but just something we do as well as we can. We learn to not strive for success, which is not under our control — but rather, to strive for excellence in all that we do. We eventually realize that there are no ordinary moments, and that we, ourselves, have a unique story to live, and maybe even to share. After our years in sport, we are not training for a meet or a game, we're training for a lifetime.

Interview Takeaway:

_____

_____

_____

_____

_____

_____

_____

_____

_____

_____

_____

College Interview: Brent (Former Duke Swimmer)

Janae– What doesn't work about your life after sport? What's missing?

Brent– I miss the constant reassurance, support and encouragement. However, because of my success in sports. I feel *as though I am almost narcissistic in my existence and feel as though everyone should pat me on the back for every little hop, skip and jump...*

Janae– Have you discovered a new dream that has you jumping out of bed each morning? Or are you surviving?

Brent– I am just surviving and trying to reach for a new dream— which is to be happy with what I have and to strive to fulfill my moral obligation to be a decent human being and do my part in life.

Janae– What dreams do you have on life support? What visions have you not yet given life to because it is not the right time, or too scary, or just a dream, or not enough money/time, or?

Brent– I want to find happiness within myself and in someone else. I am a perfectionist and am critical of others. I want pure contentment in my existence.

Interview Takeaway:

_____

_____

_____

_____

_____

_____

_____

_____

_____

_____

College Interview: Chris

(Former Quarterback- Stanford Football, current Entrepreneur, Life Coach):

Janae- What has worked about transitioning out of sport for you and the life you live today?

Chris- Sport taught me a lot about life. Competition, how to develop a game plan, preparation, team work. I could go on and on, and now as I am running my own business, it is more prevalent than ever how important the skills I learned in football are transferring to my life today. Also, it has created a tremendous bond with the guys after graduation.

Janae- What doesn't work about your life after sport? What's missing?

Chris- There is nothing like walking up to the line of scrimmage, checking the play at the line, and throwing a touchdown pass in front of a huge audience. It is a rush that can only be experienced in those moments. I wish there was a way to replicate it. What's missing is that man to man competition. I know it is still there, and it is a different sort of competition today. As I sit here and write this, I can think of ways to replicate that competition, and it was such a rush to be competing with a team of guys.

Janae- Have you discovered a new dream that has you jumping out of bed each morning? Or are you surviving?

Chris- I definitely have a dream that gets me out of bed. I think the rules of the game are different so I am acclimating myself to these new rules. I trained all my life to win on the field, and I have not completely transferred those skills into my daily life of business.

Interview Takeaway:

_____
_____
_____
_____
_____
_____
_____
_____
_____

Insights:

_____
_____
_____
_____
_____
_____
_____
_____
_____
_____
_____
_____
_____

Chapter Seven

Secret 4: Plan

When you are inspired by some great purpose, some extraordinary project, all your thoughts break their bounds. Dormant forces, faculties and talents become alive, and you discover yourself to be a greater person by far than you ever dreamed yourself to be. –Pantanjali

Whoever sows sparingly will also reap sparingly, and whoever sows bountifully will also reap bountifully. 2 Corinthians 9:6

We have tackled Identity, Vision and Foundation. Now it is time to take a goal and set up a concrete plan. I want to take some time to look at different ways of producing a result. There is an excerpt in *The Athlete Warrior* book about the impact of visualization: Olympic track athletes were hooked up to muscle testing and asked to close their eyes and visualize themselves running their race. Researchers concluded that the same muscles fibers fire as when the athlete is actually physically running the race. The brain doesn't know the difference between what it visualizes and what happens physically.[17]

Visualization and actively performing the skill are different. One is passive and the other is active. As athletes, we are wired to think that in order to produce a result, we need to

---

[17] Arnold, Alison, Ph. D. The Athlete Warrior: Creating an Unshakable Mind.p 75. www.headgamesworld.com.

work hard, and do, do, do! This is the active form. But as this study suggests, perhaps there is another way to assist success- visualization.

To illustrate this, let me ask you a question: if there were a bunch of iron shavings scattered on a table and I asked you to gather them into a pile, how would you achieve this task? Stop and think.

What is your answer?

_____

_____

_____

_____

There are actually many ways you could gather the iron shavings, and you can divide the possible techniques between the categories of passive and active.

Actively, you could roll up your sleeves and sweep them together with your hands or a broom until they are in a nice neat pile. That would absolutely work.

Another way is to get a magnet, hold it over the shavings, and watch as the shavings rapidly attract to the magnet in a pile.

The first example, of course, is the active way of producing a result. It takes more energy, work, and time. The magnet is the passive way, which is fast and relatively effortless.

So how does this relate to real-life results? Utilizing both active and passive ways to produce a result can increase your speed, power, energy, abilities, and results. It is called working smart.

As an athlete you have certainly mastered the active form. You have worked very hard for your success and produced some intense results. In fact, if you're anything like me, it might be hard for you to accept a win or triumph that came with minimal effort. The harder the struggle, the sweeter the victory.

I had to unlearn the need to struggle and overwork in order to achieve my goals. Do you? What if winning could be as effortless as holding a magnet over a table of iron shavings? Think about it. When you performed "in the zone," did it feel like really hard work, or did it feel effortless and stimulating? Sure, there is some active work that needs to be done to get to this point, or a combination of active and passive. But most of you would agree that **once you are in the zone, the work feels effortless.**

What if you could perform not only in the zone in sport, but in the zone of life? *You can!*

Some call it the sweet spot. I think of this as being in the EAC. You know, the East Australian Current, which Marlin and Dory use as their super highway to the Sydney Harbor in the movie, *Finding Nemo*. I experienced this current after our family's RV trip. Here is an example of how you can experience "the zone" in life too!

We traveled from San Diego to Canada leading couples workshops (with a toddler and an infant!). There was a storm on the coast on the way back south, homeward bound. We decided to go off course, run from the storm, and check out Central Oregon. We avoided 55 mph winds and rain to encounter a blizzard in the treacherous Cascade mountain pass - driving a twenty eight foot RV. Sweet. Upon a miraculous safe arrival and walk through town, a completely unexpected thought overtook me. I thought to myself, "We are supposed to live here!" Uproot our whole family? Leave our community and great life in San Diego? Throw away my husband's Real Estate business and start over? It made little sense. My husband was not on board. I was consumed by this notion. You can imagine how harmonious that made a marriage. I tried forcing. I shoved a lot of shameless promotion down his throat. He backed further into a corner. Finally, I aligned with the EAC, unknowingly. I went and sat on a patch of grass with my toddler and infant for a picnic, so stuck and confused, I just sat, thought and prayed. Literally like a light switch, my heart changed, I was at peace and agreed to stay in San Diego for one more year and figure it out. Enter, a current I could not stop if I tried. Everything worked out. We flourished that year. For so many reasons it was purposeful that we stayed and did not up and flee to Oregon when I wanted to. Things just worked out. Miracles happened. When we made a family "fact finding" trip back to Oregon a little over a year later, it was confirmed in all of our hearts- it is exactly where we are supposed to be. Within four months everything was swiftly taken care of and we sat back and "grabbed shell dude." We watched everything fall into place and has continued in our transition to a new state.

I experienced firsthand- when we listen, obey, and act we will experience life's greatest victories. Think of business tycoons, world champion athletes, or top performers in any field. To perform at their level becomes almost second nature to them. They have confidence in their ability. They believe they can do it and they do what it takes. They apply both passive and active techniques to producing a result. (Disclaimer: life may not always work out exactly as you plan and at the timing you have in mind, but we are focusing on a powerful way to produce a result. Insert The Rolling Stones song lyrics: "You can't always get what you want, but if you try sometimes, well you might find you get what you need.")

Here are some passive techniques to produce a desired result:

- ❖ Visualization
- ❖ Writing down goals
- ❖ Declaration
- ❖ Positive self talk
- ❖ Being your new identity
- ❖ Speaking or reading your goals regularly
- ❖ Defining and taking risks
- ❖ Creating dream boards
- ❖ Prayer
- ❖ Meditation
- ❖ Affirmations
- ❖ Creating a plan of action (goals)
- ❖ Writing vision or mission statements
- ❖ Writing your life goals
- ❖ Practicing trust and belief

Here are some active techniques to produce a desired result:

- ❖ Making marketing phone calls
- ❖ Going to practice
- ❖ Working on drills/skills
- ❖ Making marketing materials

- Giving out marketing materials
- Applying for positions
- Asking friends for opportunities/referrals
- Networking- going to events to meet people
- Writing
- Public speaking
- Joining clubs
- Studying successful people that have come before you
- Emailing
- Social media networking
- Doing physical work (such as skill, practice, labor)

Remember not to think of this as an "either/or" scenario. It won't help you to only visualize the achievements you wish to accomplish; you need to combine your visualization (and other passive techniques) with hard (active) work. The value is in the combination.

I am going to share some personal examples of a few accomplishments in my life where active and passive forms were noticeably present. The first being, my beautiful marriage: In 2003, I declared I wanted to be in a long-term committed relationship. I was ready to settle down, as they say. Though short-term recreational (or "serial") dating was satisfying in the moment and fitting for my lifestyle in New York City, I was left ultimately dissatisfied, frustrated, and obsessed with finding the right person for me. Or maybe I was more concerned with being able to love and be loved.

Either way, I was ready. Up to that point I had been unsuccessful at meeting a man who swept me off my feet. Every man I was attracted to either wasn't interested in me or clearly was not "the one" for me. I was sort of like the bird in the Dr. Seuss book, *Are You My Mother?* I would think, "What about him, or him, or maybe him?" But underneath it all, I didn't trust men. Yes I had been cheated on, more than once, but so what? I do not have to be a victim of my circumstances. And I doubted my ability to be committed and in love with one man forever. I would just get sick of them after the honeymoon stage of the relationship. Or I was scared that it would be too good to be true and he would deceive me. Needless to say, my approach to relationships was flawed.

I thought I had a fear of commitment, with some coaching and mentorship, I was able see evidence of commitment all over my life. As a gymnast, I'd clocked twenty-five hours of training a week for fifteen years. When others were going to slumber parties, to the mall or to the beach, I went to the gym; Even when I didn't want to. I finished things I started: school projects, books, college, etc. I was committed.

I made a declaration and trusted that I would find great love. I then made a list of twenty-six things I wanted in my dream man. This was very specific. It must be. I also created a project goal around this relationship that followed the steps you are about to see below. I believed it would happen. I believed I was worthy and did my best to believe I was whole and complete as I was. I could be content and trust that the perfect person for me would come in due time.

This was in November. I was in and out of a relationship that I knew was not ideal. I had to stand behind everything I said I wanted; I had to be willing to act accordingly. I finally broke that relationship off, which is inevitably uncomfortable.

The holidays came and went.

In early March, I was in Los Angeles, and a friend invited me to the one-year anniversary party of music/percussion store. I chose to go and not drive back to San Diego that night. I was early and my friends were late. I saw this guy walk in: medium, dark, and handsome! And a great presence! He happened to be single *and* the person that invited my friends to the event who in turn invited me! Did you catch that? A bit confusing, but a neat connection to get the background of this guy. We completely hit it off. I felt so incredibly comfortable with him and as many of you may have experienced, I felt like I had known him forever. From the beginning, I was able to open my heart, to love and be loved.

We have been together ever since and have created an extraordinary marriage and five incredible children. We had hurdles, but love endured. Remember that list of twenty-six things? Following our union, I located it and rated him. He met twenty-three of the twenty-six requirements. Even more remarkable is that he too had a list of what he wanted in a woman. He prayed about it and believed I was on the way. And can you imagine... both of our lists were scribbled on a little yellow sheet of paper?

No, we are not 100 percent of those things; we have our differences. But, that is why we are here together- to help each other grow. He makes me a better woman and I make him a better man. And there is great challenge in this.

Another example is my career. Following college and an impressively adventurous semester with a teammate in New Zealand, I moved to New York City and took a job selling pharmaceuticals for one of the top companies in the industry. I had a very good gig. I made money, had a company car, insurance, a computer, a cell phone, incentives, an expense account, and I was required to host physicians at only the finest restaurants in Manhattan. One would think it was pretty grand. Except for the fact that nothing compared to being an athlete, and I was not fulfilled and did not believe in the value of what I did. The company would host conferences. The marketing for certain pharmaceuticals were sport themed– treating the drug launch as a sports team– complete with sports paraphernalia to rally our "teams." A lot of resources were spent for this petty cause. During the conference, other employees would jump up, scream and shout like they had just won the World Series...at a drug conference...I didn't get it.

I didn't want to pretend I was on a sports team for a chemical in the form of a pill, I wanted to really be on a sports team again. That is how I felt at least.

In the industry as a whole, I didn't like who I was becoming, my integrity was slipping. I was use to being respected in my life, I was not accustomed to the disrespect from some physicians. Personally, I did not feel like pharmaceutical sales was what I was here on earth for.

As one of my favorite sayings goes; "Sometimes your only available transportation is a leap of faith." – Margaret Shepherd. I decided to jump. People thought I was crazy, but I resigned from that corporation. Surprisingly, the company was supportive of my decision, but without a future position or job, I moved across the country to San Diego, California. I felt the nudge to move there. I was willing to act on it. I made some poor financial decisions and took some big risks. I went into debt. Part-time personal training didn't quite pay the bills, to live solo by the beach. I enrolled in a life coaching certification program that put me even further in the red. I continued to move forward, seeking, doing the work. It took time to get my bearings and figure out what I wanted to do and how I would make a living, but in the end I managed to start my own life coaching business, and eventually join forces with someone and begin working with athletes- where I currently work very part-time hours for full time pay. I have the choice to work from home while being a homeschooling, full-time mother to my beloved kids. The risk paid off. I couldn't imagine it any other way.

My last example is; originally I wrote this book eight years ago. In that eight years, I got married, deepened my faith, grew my business, had kids, traveled, moved four times, finished half of my master's degree, and never quite finished this book. In those years I would always think, "I need to finish it." The unfinished work hung over me, not a huge burden, but something left incomplete in my life (remember, I am a completer). Then, nearly eight years later, I felt the nudge to continue this book; albeit working with current athletes in my business, I knew there were many more retired athletes who needed to hear what I had to say.

Every new year I do an exercise with my private clients as well as with my family. It is a year-end writing exercise. In the "goals for the new year" section of my own exercise, I wrote that I wanted to complete the book by March 15 of that year. I printed my list of goals and brought it with me wherever I went. On February 3, I finished the first draft of the book. And by that point I had already accomplished three other goals on that list!

The three stories I just shared with you are examples of both active and passive forms of producing a result. Passive forms are: trusting, declaring I was committed, praying, writing down goals and a plan, practicing trust and belief, being aware of messages/signs, taking risks, being bold, working in sync with my life plan (not forcing something when the timing wasn't right). Active forms are: following my plans, telling my friends and family about my plans and goals, taking actions, breaking off an undesirable relationship, communication, emailing people for support, making calls, conducting interviews, requesting time from busy/important people.

Your objective in this chapter is to bring both passive and active ways of producing a result into your plan. Are you ready to think bigger than ever before?

* First, I have one more thing to share that just happened as I was writing this in a coffee shop. A little girl named Olivia came over to me and began sniffing the flowers that were arranged in a vase on my table. She then proceeded to delicately explore the bouquet and talk to me about animals. I was talking to her about how great and caring she is with flowers, and our conversation went from there.

Five minutes later as her family was leaving, she said goodbye and excitedly ran to her parents and told them, "I now know what I want to be when I grow up. I want to be . . . I want to be . . . a Forest Manager! I want to take care of ALL the animals in the forest and help them when they get hurt!"

She was so excited about her new quest and joyously skipped out of the café. Are you kidding? When I was in the middle of writing the words, "think bigger than ever before," Olivia stepped in and did just that! It even works with six-year-olds! I would say even more so, as they have not yet developed a hardness and protection from the world. It took Olivia all of five minutes to create and share her 'life vision.'

Previously, I mentioned that you may have dreams that have been forgotten. Olivia's "Forest Manager" is what I am referring to. What is the "Forest Manager" vision of your life that you have forgotten about, or given up on? I am referring to the childhood dreams that are still desired but have been stuffed.

According to the American Society of Training and Development:

- You are 10% likely to achieve a goal if the idea came from someone else
- You are 40% likely to achieve a goal if you set a deadline
- You are 50% likely to achieve a goal if you write a plan of action
- You are 65% likely to achieve a goal if you declare your intentions to someone else
- You are 95% likely to achieve a goal if you allow someone else to hold you accountable for your progress[18]

---

[18] www.astd.org. America Society of Training and Development. Retrieved 2005.

Leadership IQ, a leadership development and research company, did a study regarding goal setting techniques. They discovered that employees who were pushed past their comfort zone had twenty nine percent higher engagement. They also discovered some predictors of whether a person's goals were going to help them maximize their potential.

Predictors include:

- I can vividly picture how great it will feel when I achieve my goals.
- I will have to learn new skills to achieve my assigned goals for this year.
- My goals are absolutely necessary to help this company.
- I actively participated in creating my goals for this year.[19]

I want to stretch you to think big. Tim Ferriss talks about "Dreamlining," which is attaching timelines to what most would consider dreams. When we think of dreams, we think of a desire somewhere out there that we would surely love to have become a reality but do not believe it possible. The "New Rich," do believe it possible and therefore attach a timeline and defined steps.

Tim quotes Samuel Beckett, "Ever tried. Ever failed. No matter. Try again. Fail again. Fail better. You won't believe what you can accomplish by attempting the impossible with

---

[19]http://www.prweb.com/releases/2010/04/prweb3825384.htm?PID=4003003 "New Leadership IQ Paper Asks, Are SMART Goals Dumb?" Murphy, Mark. Retrieved February 6, 2014.

the courage to repeatedly fail better."[20]

So let's get started. Let's create a **Personal Plan (PP)- complete with a goal, visual and timeline.** What do you want? You may want to refer to your Personal Vision List from Secret 2: Vision chapter. I had you create the vision list first to ignite your dreaming and get out there. Now that you have worked your Vision and Foundation, you have a better idea of what you really want and where you still might be stuck. Is there an item on your PIL you have not been able to tackle yet? Choose one goal that you want to work on now. **A goal that, when accomplished, would be even more fulfilling than being an athlete!** What is your biggest challenge that you want to break through? What do you feel like you were put on earth to do? What would rock your world? **Keep in mind that people tend to overestimate what they can do in a year and underestimate what they can do in ten years.**

Step 1: Determine Your Goal.

My Goal is:

_____

_____

_____

_____

_____

Step 2: Visual.

Picture vividly how great it will feel when you achieve your

---

[20]Ferriss, Timothy. The 4-Hour Workweek: Escape 9-5, Live Anywhere, and Join the New Rich. Crown Publishing Group, 2007. p 43 & p 46.

goal; this will maximize your potential to achieve it. Write at least a paragraph, and let it flow. Write as many pages of your visual as you wish. What will life look like for you when this goal is accomplished? Write as if you have already achieved your goal. For example, "I wake up in the morning and jump out of bed, excited about my work." Not, "I will wake up..." Once your goal is accomplished, what are you experiencing? What is life like for you now? What thoughts, feelings, emotions are you having, who is sharing in the excitement? How do you celebrate?

Recall the example of the Olympic athletes visualizing; they ran the race in their minds and their vision of running activated similar muscle fibers as actually running. Set up your visual, and then live into it. I do like the saying, "Shoot for the moon, you may land on a star." My gymnastics team never won a National Championship, but we competed at NCAA Championships every year- we landed on a star.

Write a visual specific to your goal:

_____

_____

_____

_____

_____

_____

_____

_____

_____

_____

_____

_____

Step 3: Winning Timeline.

The intention is not to look at the top of the mountain and start climbing. That would be overwhelming and paralyzing. How do you eat an elephant? One bite at a time. Let's chunk it down, just like you did for any athletic goal.

When my gymnastics team's goal was to win Nationals in April of that year, we broke the larger goal down into shorter-term goals or steps, such as:

- ❖ Step 1- Have a strong and healthy lineup on each event with backups by December 15th
- ❖ Step 2- Reach a 195+ team score at first meet
- ❖ Step 3- Maintain a top ten ranking during the season
- ❖ Step 4- Win Regionals, which would qualify us for Nationals
- ❖ Step 5- Qualify in top three of our session to advance to Super Six
- ❖ Step 6- Compete for and win the national title

Now it is your turn. What are the steps to your goal? Write them in order.

(You do not need 10, this is an outline. Note: your final step will be your end result/goal.)

Step 1-_____

Step 2-_____

Step 3-_____

Step 4-_____

Step 5-_____

Step 6-_____

Step 7-_____

Step 8-_____

Step 9-_____

Step 10-_____

Step 4: Action Plan.

Break it down even further. What actions (passive and active) will you need to take to get to each step?

In our gymnastics team's example, the action plan included:

Step 1: Have a strong and healthy lineup on each event with backups by December 15th

Actions to achieve this:

1. Practice 5 days a week for 3-4 hours
2. Strength train in the mornings
3. Declare and write goals, both personal and for the team
4. Write out cue routines (mental routines)

5. Practice cue routines daily
6. Start with basic routine to build strength and endurance and slowly add half routines and then full routines
7. Do drills
8. Be consistent in training and pressure routines
9. Choose lineup based on performance and readiness

Now do the same for all of your steps. Remember, you do not need ten steps and ten action items for each; this is just a general guide. Break down the number of steps you listed with appropriate actions.

- **Step 1:** (actions to achieve step)

1. _____

2. _____

3. _____

4. _____

5. _____

6. _____

7. _____

8. _____

9. _____

10. _____

- **Step 2:**

    1. _____

    2. _____

    3. _____

    4. _____

    5. _____

    6. _____

    7. _____

    8. _____

    9. _____

    10. _____

- **Step 3:**

    1. _____

    2. _____

3. _____

4. _____

5. _____

6. _____

7. _____

8. _____

9. _____

10. _____

- **Step 4:**

    1. _____

    2. _____

    3. _____

    4. _____

    5. _____

    6. _____

    7. _____

8. _____

9. _____

10. _____

- **Step 5:**

  1. _____

  2. _____

  3. _____

  4. _____

  5. _____

  6. _____

  7. _____

  8. _____

  9. _____

  10. _____

- **Step 6:**

  1. _____

2. _____

3. _____

4. _____

5. _____

6. _____

7. _____

8. _____

9. _____

10. _____

- **Step 7:**

1. _____

2. _____

3. _____

4. _____

5. _____

6. _____

7. _____

8. _____

9. _____

10. _____

- **Step 8:**

    1. _____

    2. _____

    3. _____

    4. _____

    5. _____

    6. _____

    7. _____

    8. _____

    9. _____

    10. _____

- **Step 9:**

  1. _____
  2. _____
  3. _____
  4. _____
  5. _____
  6. _____
  7. _____
  8. _____
  9. _____

- **Step 10:**

  1. _____
  2. _____
  3. _____
  4. _____
  5. _____

6. _____

7. _____

8. _____

9. _____

10. _____

Step 5: Celebrate your winnings!

Celebrate, reward yourself, and find ways to make this fun. We do not celebrate our progress enough in life. We seem to focus much more on what we lack than on how far we have come. After you have written out your steps and actions for each step, give yourself a reward. It can be monetary or non-monetary, making sure it is a financially responsible choice: new shirt, movie night, coffee, dinner out, fifteen minutes of nothing time, nap, social media time, itunes album, thirty minutes of video games, new book, weekend away, card night, massage, play night with the kids, trip to a favorite beach, favorite food, manicure, new outfit, new electronic, hour of T.V., cruise, week off from work, trip, massage chair, visit to a local museum, gym membership, tickets to an event, and so on.

When I was first starting my business, I had to make marketing calls and I couldn't find one ounce of motivation. I would have rather cleaned my toilet. I called my husband and he told me that if I made the calls he would bring me home a prize. I had no idea what the prize was—it could've been a green gum ball—but I was suddenly motivated! I picked up that phone, dialed away, felt great, and was suddenly filled with motivation! Motivation that snowballed into more action and more possibility.

This is no different than athletic awards ceremonies and banquets. These are rewards for our efforts/achievements. Even outside of the world of sports you will see rewards in every aspect of life. When I worked for corporate America, my company would spend an absurd amount of money sending rewards to their sales team, such as a Footlocker gift card saying, "We are going to hit the ground running." We love rewards and we keep working for them. One of my favorite parts of the Olympic Games is seeing the celebration of a winning performance; you know- the knee slides, pointing to the sky screaming, being carried to the podium, dropping to the ground, hugging mom, or the ecstatic jumps for joy and the medal ceremony. I absolutely love the celebration of performance.

Share Opp- @transitionwhatnow post how you are going to reward yourself and #ismellvictory.

Movie to watch:

* ★ *About Schmidt* (2002) or *Same Kind of Different as Me (2017)*. We all have a desire to make a difference in the world.

* ★ Give yourself 3 points for writing out the steps for your goal.___

★ Give yourself 1 point if you watched the movie._____

Celebrity Interview: Kerry McCoy

Janae– Kerry McCoy is a two time Olympian and two time NCAA National Champion Heavyweight wrestler. He was a Team USA wrestler for nine years. He has multiple 1st, 2nd, 3rd, and 4th place finishes at World Championships and international tournaments. He placed 7th and 5th in the Olympic games.

Janae– I know for you specifically, you made the transition from athlete to coach. You stayed in the sport of wrestling and transitioned into assistant at Lehigh and now head coach at Stanford University (currently Maryland). How was it transitioning from athlete to coach?

Kerry– Well for me, the situation is not as cut and dry: athlete-coach, because during seven years of my coaching career I was a competitive athlete. Through 1997–1998 when I made my first World Team I was coaching and still competing. Through both Olympics, I was an assistant coach. It wasn't as sharp as it is for most athletes where they compete compete compete and then go to coaching. My transition was college athlete– college coach. The same time I was in college I was an international athlete and now I am completely out of competition. And that is really where the transition would be from competitive athlete/coach to only coach. The transition has been great. I love every day. Every day is another opportunity to do something great.

Janae– Yes just knowing you personally I have watched you transition from one to the next and it seems pretty seamless for *you. What do you think has made it seamless for you? The coaching? Your level of success?*

Kerry- *I think it is everything. Everything I got out of the sport and put into the sport as an athlete I am trying to trying to put that back into it as a coach. When you do, it is pretty easy. Basically I know I have had a lot of good coaches through my career and the things that they helped teach me and shared with me, that knowledge, I want to share with my guys. It is just kind of like that transition of, you know, from point A to point B. Them being point A and me being point B. I move them onto point B (which is my guys I coach now).*

Janae- *Neat way to put it. Experiencing peak performance, being in the flow or the zone or whatever you like to call, it is something that a lot of athletes seem to miss when they retire from their sport. Do you think that being in the zone is something you can experience in life beyond sport?*

Kerry- *Oh- without a doubt. Without a doubt. For example, as a coach when things just click and you're out there and you just seem like every time there is a situation and you are right on top of it. In the business world you seem to know just when to make that call, when to make that sale, when to make whatever it is you are doing, the words just flow out. In life in general, you know, when you are in the zone it is like everything is clicking and everything is going as you would envision it to be as perfect. Perfect opportunity for example. So it definitely happens in other areas. If you didn't experiences it in athletics you probably wouldn't recognize it as such, outside of athletics.*

Janae- *Got it. Some athletes have the performance of their lifetime and reach their goals and retire at the pinnacle of their* *career. They win a gold medal in the Olympic Games, or win World Championships, Super Bowl, or NCAA Championships or whatever it is for that person's individual goals. I would say most athletes retire having not yet reached that ultimate goal or personal best they set out for. A lot of athletes seem to have trouble with that. Myself, personally, with being injured before being able to reach all of my goals, is a lot more challenging transition when there is still some incomplete business left in sport. For you, I know that your ultimate goal was to be a gold medalist at the Olympic Games. Having come so close and not achieving that exact goal how does that impact your transition?*

Kerry– *Kind of funny I had conversation today with another guy that was a two time world champion and has never won the Olympics. He said; "To this day, I still wish I would have won the Olympics." And it bothers him to this day. He was a competitive athlete back in '80. And he would have probably been an Olympic champ if United States didn't boycott. It is one of those things with your ultimate goal, that if you never quite reached it, you will always no matter what, you will always say... "Man I wish I would have, or I could or should have or whatever." But I take comfort because I know deep down, I mean I could have made a different adjustment in a match or made this move instead of that. But ultimately where I have comfort is that I know that I did everything in my power to give me the opportunity and give me a chance to go up there and perform.*

To have a peak performance when it counts is only a handful of people that are able to do that. Obviously in the sport of wrestling where there are ten gold medals. In 1996 there were eight and in 2000/2004 there were seven gold medals. So the opportunity to be an Olympic champ in the last twelve years has only been twenty-five gold medals. With all the athletes that compete in the sport throughout the world, throughout the years, there have only been twenty-five in the last twelve years that have won Olympic gold medals. There are a lot of people that aren't gonna win. It doesn't mean that you aren't necessarily the best, but on that day you weren't the best that you could have been or you weren't the best that you should have been.

What I take comfort in is the fact that I know that I train harder, smarter, than anyone else in the world. When it came down to it it just wasn't meant to be. That's one thing [that is hard] but yet everyday I think about the Olympic Games, both of them. "What if or if I would have done this or if I would have tried this or I was going to try this... "Maybe I would have won, but it wasn't because of a lack of preparation or a lack of training or a lack of desire. I think that is the difference that helped me move forward and that is one of the things that hold people back. If someone knew that they cut corners and didn't give it their all, that can be a lot more difficult to deal with than the person that did everything right and it just didn't happen.

Janae- Along those lines, a challenge I see that athletes face is with vision. An athlete has always had a vision for a performance or a season and we knew what we wanted to do and what kind of action plan we needed. We had a coach, a team, and all the other support structures together. How important do you think it is for a retired athlete to have a vision for their life?

Kerry- It is just as important when you are retired as it is when you are competing. You need to have a goal, you need to have a plan. Nothing is accomplished without a goal, without a plan. Nothing in anything. From the plan...is it more strict more *regimented? Or is it more loose or what? Ultimately you can't just wake up in the morning and just blow through the day and see what happens. You have to know, okay I'm going to get up, I'm going to take a shower, I'm going to brush my teeth, I'm going to go to work. At work I'm going to do whatever it is that you gotta do, you need a plan. How structured are the plans, how strict are the plans, you gotta vary with each individual. But you need to have a plan, a vision, the goal, the what you want to accomplish. Because if you don't have something to shoot for why are you even doing what you're doing?*

Janae- *Thanks. Any advice for athletes today for facing the challenge of leaving their sport and going onto new endeavors?*

Kerry- *I would say like I said before, take confidence in what you have accomplished. Stay confident in your preparation for that because it's going to be hard to be satisfied with not being completely successful (as far as reaching every goal you set out for). Even some champions are upset that they won the match by a point instead of by five points. We are always seeking perfection and there is no perfection. There is only one perfect person who ever walked this earth... so everybody else is going to fall short. So just take confidence in the fact that you have done everything in your power. And give yourself a chance of achieving goals. When you are ready to move on, move on because you are ready to move on don't move on because it is "your time," move on because you're ready to move on. If you still have that desire and that opportunity...because that other thing is regret. That's one thing I've thought about. If you look back and say, "Man I wish I would have just given it one more try."... that is going to haunt you even more than trying and failing, well not really failing, but not reaching your goals.*

There are so many athletes out there that get out too early just as there's some athletes stay in too long. I think the ones that get out too early and don't give themselves a chance they have a lot more regret than those that go a little bit longer because then at least they say oh you know I tried it wasn't meant to be, I was a little past my prime or whatever. The athlete that sits back and says, "Man I wish I would have tried out for that next Olympic team." That will eat at you a lot more than if you made the team and didn't win or tried and didn't make it. At least you know you gave it a shot.

Janae- *How has your faith carried you?*

Kerry- *It is everything. I mean I wouldn't be here without the grace of God. I owe it all to Him...to have me here and giving me the opportunity to do the things I do. Like I said, I wouldn't be here without Him. It is very important. My spirituality is one thing that helped me go through my career. I know all of this that we go through is just... well nothing, because in reality we have a greater prize, a far greater prize waiting for us. So this is just a space saver in the time being, so I know that having that in my mind and taking confidence in that really makes a difference. I know that I have a far greater prize than any gold medal could ever give.*

Janae- *Research shows that staying in your sport in some way has made the adjustment easier. It seems in your case that staying in wrestling and being an impactful head coach has helped. It is your success as an athlete that has led you to this coaching position where you are so focused on the sport of wrestling; And like you said, helping other guys reach the level of success that you had. Is there any moment in this role of coach, now, that you just wish you were on the mat again as an athlete,* *rather than a coach?*

Kerry– *[laughing]. Not too often. That is another reason why God confirmed my decision to move on. Everyday I may wish that I had... or wish I were an Olympic champ... or I wish I had the opportunity I wish I was taking advantage of my opportunity, well not necessarily to take advantage of them, but I wish I would have won. I will come in and roll around with the guys and I'm like "Hey it would be nice to go out there and wrestle right now and challenge your world title." But I am not like "Oh my gosh I really want to get back in there!" It is more "ahh ya know..." If this was a World Championship Tournament right now and I was wrestling it would be pretty cool but it's not and I don't dwell on it because obviously I, going back to that regret, I gave it everything I had put my best foot forward and got the result that was meant to be. If I honestly really had a desire I would do it again because I'm still physically able, capable to do it. That's why I know I am confident in my decision to walk away from this sport. I always joke with people, the one thing with wrestling is that you actually walk away from the sport. Some other athletes they have to use some assistance.*

Janae– *Yes...Hobble! One thing that is very important for ex-athletes to understand is there are greater wins ahead. Many athletes I see today view life– as an athlete, as the glory days or that was as good as it is going to get. What would you recommend for these athletes to see the best is yet to come?*

Kerry– *First they have to be open to that. They have to be open to the fact that yeah the best is yet to come. Every athlete has different things that motivate them. I can't imagine how I may feel because I don't have any kids but how will it be to have your first child born? Or to have your child succeed in something. Or a* *family member you know, do something really great. Things like that. Or for me as a coach when my athletes have gone and had success, the joy that that brings me. I mean there are different things that will bring out incredible amounts of joy. Each of them is different so it's just a matter of what you commit to. Be open to the idea that the best is yet to come. That the glory days, you know, people say "college is the best four years of your life." And it is, but the next step has to occur, you can't stay in college forever. You're going to have to be open to whatever may come and just realized that yeah for some people facing that is at 22, for some it is 32, some peoples it is 42. But you know God willing you have a long life to live. And there are incredible things that can happen. There are athletes that have had family and kids and do that while they're competing. Who knows what that next step is going to be. I can imagine athletes that have kids that go on and do a similar sport and have similar success, that has to be an incredible feeling. So it is just a matter of different perspective. You just have to be open and aware especially. There is other stuff out there you have to be open to it.*

Janae– I think being a gymnast, let's say you have a child and that child chooses a similar sport that you did. I have seen a lot of parents live vicariously through their children, projecting their unresolved issues. So that's why I think it is so important to have the attitude and the mentality that you have, Kerry. You are complete with that you gave it your all and you gave it your best. There is nothing, I don't believe, that you would impart on your child who may grow up and be a wrestler. You will not live vicariously through them rather just support them in being their best.

Kerry– Exactly.

Janae- That is extremely important for former athletes and parents to understand when their kids are going through their sport as well.

Kerry- You asked some good questions, I really appreciate the insight it created because it really gave me a chance to express myself in a way that I couldn't do just by talking. When you have the right questions, answers come out a lot easier.

Janae- Thank you again.

UPDATE:

Head Coach at the University of Maryland, 2008-present
Married, a son and a daughter (his son is wrestler)
2014 induction into the National Wrestling Hall of Fame as a Distinguished Member

Interview Takeaway:

_____
_____
_____
_____
_____
_____
_____
_____
_____

Celebrity Interview: Amy Tedder

Janae- I am here with Amy Tedder who is a former gymnast. She is 17 years old. Actually she has gone through a transition out of sport that many cannot even fathom -a very unique situation. I know you have been an inspiration to the gymnastics community, Amy, for your perseverance. Your reason for not being able to compete is so powerful I would rather you tell your story if you wouldn't mind sharing with us.

Amy- Okay well on October 21, 2005 I was diagnosed with Hodgkin's lymphoma. It was a pretty sudden thing. It was hard for the doctors to diagnose and so it was a very big surprise. The doctors were surprised. I was surprised. Everyone was surprised when they told me I had cancer, because the doctors didn't even realize it until a result from pathology came in. Previous to that I have been a gymnast for about eleven years.

That summer I had gone to Junior Olympic Nationals in California for gymnastics for level 10. That was one of my biggest goals in my gymnastics career. So that was a highlight of my career. When I got back from that I was going into my Junior year of high school and my goal has always been to get a college scholarship for gymnastics. And so that's what I was working toward.

Junior year was a big year for college recruiting in gymnastics. I was excited to work hard and get new skills. I started to notice pains in my sternum. At first I didn't give it that much attention because any athlete has aches and pains all the time, that is part of athletics. But it started to get worse and the lump started to form in my sternum. That was a little abnormal. So my mom and I decided to go to the orthopedic doctor that we knew really well. Unfortunately, he didn't really know what was going on he just kinda said "Well you know it looks like a tumor but I don't really know." He ordered tests and stuff and sent us to Hershey Medical Center in Hershey, PA. They did more tests, scans and blood work and things like that. The doctors there met about it – had a little meeting about my case. They were 95% sure it was not cancer, that it was stress fracture in my sternum.

That was great news for us to hear, then! Well, it wasn't good news for me. But my parents were relieved but then they said I was going to have to have major surgery on my sternum– clean it up, fix it, so that I would be able to eventually go back to gymnastics. Because at this point I wasn't going to be able to train it was so weak and it could break further. So then on October 16th I had the surgery. Then they said that it was going to be about a six month recovery so I was really really upset because that was going to totally knock out my whole junior year of competition for gymnastics. I wouldn't be able to train for six months! I would start to be able to come back end of my junior year. That was a total blow to my gymnastics career but I thought, you know, I will be able to come back. I'll just have to make it work because I still want to pursue my dream of a scholarship in college.

On October 21st ...five days after my surgery we got the call from the results from pathology. The doctor basically just said we thought it might be an infection or something but we got the results from pathology in and it's cancer and there's no doubt about it... definitely cancer; it is Hodgkin's disease. We were just blown away by that. All my worries and all about not being able to compete in my gymnastics career were placed to the back burner and I was like "Wow I have to fight for my life at this point."

So I started chemotherapy on November 7th. I couldn't train anymore through chemo mostly because of my surgery I couldn't do a thing. But once six months of recovery hit, my body was just still too weak, too depleted from chemo to go back. I had eight months of therapy eight cycles– it took eight months to get through. Once I was done with chemotherapy, my last day was May 16th 2006; I decided I wanted to try to go back to gymnastics and see if I could do it– maybe compete my senior year. I knew I wasn't going to do it in college because when you lose a year in level 10, in gymnastics that's a big step to get back in it. You can't really go back to where you were in just a year. I tried to go back into the gym. I started to train again and just try to get back to it. I really couldn't.

After about a month of training and doing things it was too hard on my body. The doctors weren't sure if it was the best thing because originally from the cancer that created lesions in my bones the lymphoma spread to my bones. It's just kinda like holes in my bones. They have been keeping an eye on those throughout my treatment and everything. And after I was done with my treatment, conditions were still there they just weren't getting worse which was good but there were still lesions in my bones. So I was thinking, "Is that going to be hazardous? Am I going to be more susceptible to breaking bones and stuff?" They said they didn't really know. The only way to know is to try it and if I break a bone we will know you are not ready to go back. So I said okay well I will try.

I was just having too much pain and stuff so I just decided that I didn't really want to wait until I broke something to see that I wasn't ready. I wasn't going to be able to go back. I kind of just decided to explore other options my senior year. It was my last year and I wanted to maybe try to do a school sport. And just be more involved with school activities and things that I have never been able to do before because gymnastics was so time consuming- pretty much the only thing I could do. I would train for 30 hours a week and some weekends and stuff. It was a hard decision to make because I still miss gymnastics and I love it and I always will.

But now I'm in track so that is fun. It is a new experience with a new team. So that is pretty much where I am at right now.

Janae- Whoaaa. So you were going through this at about age 16, at a pretty young age. Have you been able to wrap your head around this?

Amy- Yeah. I definitely do. You know when I first started going through this it was just so hard to look at it positively.

Janae- Sure! I know personally, I take life for granted. I hear stories of those with... usually it is a life threatening illness where they are faced with a reality that they might not take another breath. With someone who hasn't really faced something like that, I haven't experienced the preciousness and urgency of life. It is something that I try to feel, "This is urgent!" I do appreciate many many many things in my life. However I am wondering for you, a person who has faced that possibility, especially at 16 years old; how has that changed your appreciation of being alive each day?

Amy- Mainly, you know, as soon as I was diagnosed it hit me like "wow!" Because I really didn't have any symptoms or reasons to think that I had cancer at all. I was diagnosed in stage four right when I was diagnosed. There are four stages of lymphoma. And so I mean, I was the worst point and I didn't, I had no reason to think, I mean that summer- I had cancer and I competed at nationals, you know? And so I was just hit with- we are not guaranteed tomorrow! Nothing is guaranteed. Life is temporary. I have to make sure that I am living it to the fullest. Definitely and that is why I feel blessed with time. It does give you a perspective like nothing else can. I wish that I could impress that upon other people and just give them that mindset that I have been able to gain.

Sometimes I forget, you know, I get caught up in all of the everyday stuff. But I kind of remind myself that I need to remember that the little problems in life don't really matter. And I need to be living out my life as much as I can because you never know what is going to happen. I guess I have a different perspective than most 17 year olds because of going through something like that. I think anybody who goes through cancer has that mindset. But I can remember that and I think I will for the rest of my life. It really helps you live and appreciate things more. But I appreciate my friends and family so much more because they were so supportive of me throughout. It just meant so much to me. I knew I loved my friends and family but showing them how much I love them is more important to me, now that I realize things like that are what really are important. That is some of the things I learned. I learned a lot of lessons in that eight months.

Janae- I was just reading a book about something similar, a guy who was a little older, but he got cancer. He went through his entire chemotherapy and was a really optimistic person; shaving his head before chemo then dipping it in gold sparkles and running around the house in his underwear calling himself "Chemo-man...Cheemo Maan!" That was his attitude going into chemo. And he went through his cycles. Four months later, when he went into his doctor's appointment, he was given results that he was back into stage four cancer. As a physician himself he knew that this quick- fast resurge of cancer was basically a death sentence. He knew it. So he went home and he called his friends. One of his friends was a pastor. He called him just to share and they balled. They cried for hours. The pastor himself was in complete denial and couldn't even get to prayer he was just so upset about this. The next morning the pastor awoke thinking "This can't be... there has got to be another way." That morning at 6 a.m., he got a call from his friend who had cancer to tell him the news that he had actually received incorrect lab results and it was somebody else who hadn't even received chemo yet and that he was in fact cured and in remission!"

Amy- Oh Wow! Oh my gosh.

Janae- Yes, what was so inspiring about the story is that he proceeds to say how his life and going through cancer- the possibility of death but then when he had that one night really in the face of death. He spoke about touching his kids, hugging them and his wife and spending time with them. He couldn't express that enough. How that was his everything. You know that cliche' 'don't sweat the small stuff' but it was all those little things that were stressful, none of that was important anymore. Even in a relationship that we tend to argue about. Or with friends, or in sports. You stub a toe or break a finger, it is ok. Just keep on moving.

Amy- Yes.

Janae- I am sure you have that perspective because you get that small stuff doesn't really matter sometimes.

Amy- I am the type of person that always sweat the small stuff.

I'm kind of a worrier, or I was. You know, grades and stuff in high school I would get so stressed out over that and the little things in daily life. I was so worried about my gymnastics career because that was so important to me at that point. When you get a diagnosis like that, it is like "oh my gosh!" It really puts things in perspective as just not important right now. If I have a test tomorrow at school, it is not going to make or break my life. It has helped me a lot to be more relaxed about stuff and appreciate things that do matter. Not to worry about the things that don't matter. Not to say that I never worry about little things because I think we all do.

Janae– That is great! Few will have to face something like you did; but for athletes who may be facing a similar situation as you, such as forced retirement from sport. Which can be due to injury which is very common, being cut, an illness or something as serious as cancer; do you have any words of wisdom or advice for them?

Amy– Well, just that when you are an athlete and you've been in a sport your whole life and you are going towards a certain goal it seems like having to end your athletic career is the worst thing that could possibly happen to you. But it is not. There are ways that you can still find fulfillment other than that sport. You know how that saying goes, 'When one door closes another door opens,' I have found that to be true. You just have to keep the right mindset. It is a hard thing to do... easier said than done. Ending your career is not ending your opportunities. It is hard to get to that point where you can see beyond the end of your career or your illness, but there are definitely other things you can pursue. I am looking forward to college. I might play intramural volleyball or something that I've always wanted to do. And I'm just going to enjoy being in college. I can actually having a life, ya know? There are other things to look at positively even if you can't do your sport you love.

Janae– So great. Do you have any idea what you wanna be when you grow up? [laughing].

Amy– Yes I want to be a psychologist. That is what I want to major in. Not sure where I'm going to go to college yet. It is between University of North Carolina if I don't get in there I will go to Louisiana State University. I am excited to see what the future holds for me. I have plans for my future but I have learned that God's plans are bigger. You have to be flexible with your plans. I had my whole life planned out at 16 and in one second it was totally messed up.

Janae– Anything else you would like to add?

Amy– No I pretty much talked your head off I think.

Janae– Thank you very much Amy, you are an inspiration.

Amy– You are very welcome!

UPDATE:

Amy– My health now is wonderful! I think my doctor even uses the word "thriving." This spring I ran the 10 mile Cherry Blossom race in DC and have signed up for a few smaller races this fall. I was a part of the LSU club rowing team and have continued to pursue the sport by joining a community crew in DC called Capital Rowing Club.

Amy– I attended Louisiana State University and earned a

Bachelor of Science in Psychology. I plan to apply to graduate school this fall in hopes of attending in the fall of 2015 and attaining a Masters in Organizational Development.

Amy– *Currently I am a teacher at a private elementary school in Washington, DC called Beauvoir. It is the National Cathedral Elementary School and in the fall I will be teaching 1st grade.*

Amy– *My advice to athletes forced into premature retirement is this; your health comes first. Take care of your body while you're young because that may give you the opportunity to participate in new and different sports when you're older. Retiring early from gymnastics opened the door for me to play intramural volleyball and row for a club team in college– neither of which I could've predicted I would get involved in. Early retirement from the sport you love doesn't mean you give up being an athlete, you'll* **ALWAYS** *be an athlete no matter what sport you pursue.*

Interview Takeaway:

_____
_____
_____
_____
_____
_____
_____
_____
_____
_____

College Interview: Ellen

(Former Penn State University All-American gymnast, current Physical Medicine and Rehabilitation Doctor, Author, Wife, Mother)

Janae- Rate your level of joy, power and satisfaction on a scale of 1- 10 (1 being head in the sand, 10 being I jump for joy daily)

Ellen- a.) as a competitive athlete- 8 to 9
b.) now–Internship 4, I expect that next year it will be closer to 7
Janae- What doesn't work about your life after sport? What's missing?

Ellen- I really miss the physical challenge- the feeling of fatigue in your muscles after the hardest workout you've ever done. Also the excitement of trying new skills- there is some of this in learning new procedures, but it's scarier since people's lives are depending on my performance, and although it's technical, it's not as fun. Calls can be physically demanding, but I don't feel the same sense of accomplishment at the end as I do with physical exercise- maybe it's because I haven't done anything "good" for my body, just for others.

Janae- Have you discovered a new dream that has you jumping out of bed each morning? Or are you surviving.

Ellen- A little bit of both- I am currently just surviving. I am in a profession that thrives on delayed gratification, and the many years still left before I'm doing what I want are starting to get frustrating. I am optimistic that when I'm able to create a sports medicine practice, including invasive procedures, sports specific training/exercise prescription and cover National team/Olympic events, I will be as close to jumping out of bed every morning as I can be.

UPDATE:

Janae- Here we are nearly 10 years later. What have you accomplished in this time?

Ellen- Professionally: In the past 10 years, I completed internship, residency and fellowship training. I got my dream job - academic sports medicine and created a women's sports program at Northwestern. I also received a 3-year, $300,000 grant from the National Institutes of Health to research the influence of sex hormones on the increased risk of ACL injuries in females compared to males. I have had approximately 10 peer-reviewed manuscripts published along with several book chapters. I was recently asked to write a textbook on Sex Differences in Sports Medicine.

Personally: I am blessed to have continued to be married to my wonderful husband and we now have two children and an 8 year old dog. In addition, I have maintained wonderful relationships with my parents, sisters, extended family and friends.

Janae- How has your experience as an athlete propelled your future?

Ellen- I believe my athletic experience has led me to have a strong work ethic and drive to achieve my goals.

Janae- Research shows this transition is the most paralyzing for athletes who experience involuntary retirement. Which makes *sense. I would also say that this challenge has a window of around 1 -10 years post retirement. What is your advice for athletes transitioning out of sport today who are not yet at this stage of acceptance?*

Ellen– Involuntary retirement is interesting. I would think that this mainly applies to someone who retires against his/her will, mostly due to injury. However, I retired because I was finished with my college eligibility and "gymnastics is not a lifelong sport." I am grateful that I knew my retirement was coming and that I had time to prepare, but it still didn't truly feel voluntary. However, knowing that it was coming enabled me to focus on the present and my goals during my final season more intensely than I had before. I also took time to reflect on the things I loved most about my sport and being an athlete (feeling of accomplishment, teammates, working hard) and tried to enjoy them on a daily basis. Finally, my advice is to pick something else or another way to challenge yourself. It doesn't have to be as big or all-consuming as your sport, but a new physical activity or goal can help maintain a sense of purpose if this feels lacking without your sport.

Interview Takeaway:

_____

_____

_____

_____

_____

_____

_____

_____

_____

Insights:

Chapter Eight

Secret 5: Structure and Support

Nobody ever made it to the Olympics without a coach.
Why would you try to win your best life without one?
–Debbie Ford

It is important for everyone to have a support system, and for former athletes who are accustomed to an abundance of support, it is tough to even function without it. Our whole lives we have been told where to show up, what to do, when to do it, and how we should do it. We did not even have to think about too much other than playing our sport, which was by design. One of the challenges I found in retirement was the freedom of choice, believe it or not. When I entered the "real world" as an ex-athlete, I acted a bit like a rebellious teenager . . . only I was in my mid-twenties. I had followed such a year round rigorous schedule for so long that when I was on my own, I wanted nothing to do with full weekly schedules and meticulously structured days. After I resigned from corporate America and created my own company, I demanded a lot of flexibility. I insisted on no alarm clock, getting up whenever my eyelids opened, taking Fridays off as "Janae day," not being bound to a commitment in case something popped up that I wanted to do, you get the point. And though this relaxed lifestyle felt good at the time, I knew deep down that my aversion to structure was holding me back from being my best self and achieving my highest goals. Sure, I want these freedoms in my life, but only as a result of setting myself up financially, living purposefully, and being my best. Can you see the difference?

As athletes, we were productive and successful because of the structure of training and competition schedules. Today— years later, after I started my business, have a husband and five kids —my life is more structured, and I have learned to employ a similar discipline I learned in sport, into my career and daily life. Of course, everyone is different; After your retirement, you might thrive right away in a career or lifestyle that is completely structured. Some of you may be more like me (rebelling structure), or somewhere in the middle. What I do know is that a flexible routine, flexible structure, and support are essential to my own success and happiness. I emphasize flexible because I believe flexibility is required in life; when we get too rigid, joy and fulfillment can get lost.

Back to when I was first starting my business and hadn't yet realized the importance of daily routines and scheduling, I got to a point where I didn't even want to get out of bed in the mornings. I didn't have any appointments in the morning and there was nothing calling me forward and onward in my life. My schedule was pretty empty. I had freedom to go to the beach or do whatever I wanted. Of course, I did not have the financial luxury to do that daily, so that created some restriction. And when I did something that was unproductive, I would feel overwhelmed with guilt. So, was I really free? I felt stuck in the muck! I was more like a stagnant swamp than the powerfully flowing river that we were created to be.

Finally, one day I decided that if I want to go after my dreams it was time to welcome support and structure into my life. *Iron sharpens iron, and one man sharpens another.* (Proverbs 27:17). I always knew I did my best work in a structured and supported environment. I was ready to dig myself out of the muck and bring purpose and energy back to my daily life. The desire and decision were key factors. I then decided and acted on getting my financial life back on track.

In one and a half months I quadrupled my income (I wasn't starting from six-figures, but quadrupled was quadrupled). Once I generated some momentum, I was unstoppable. In the past, when I was resisting structure, I struggled to build my business. But this time it felt effortless, and even fun. It is really empowering to produce results and play big. I loved the structure and the support systems I used which were similar to this book. The experience of resisting structure, feeling the impact, and getting into gear helped bring me to where I am today.

So, what does a healthy support system look like? You can custom design it to work for you. In sport, athletes have: coaches, teammates, athletic trainers, strength trainers, doctors, academic advisors, sports psychologists, sponsors, managers, agents, and people who wash uniforms, pack training gear, plan travel, and prepare meals. We had a strict schedule and mandatory practices, study halls, strength training, meetings, volunteer work, travel, community service, and game days. We had consequences if we did not show up, and we had team members and coaches to answer to. We had internal and external motivation to be there. We had a set weekly schedule. All of these things were in place so we could focus our energy on our game. It worked.

You don't necessarily need this level of support and structure to be functional in your life after sport. The levels of structure and support that work for you will depend on your level of rebellion or resistance to structure, and the intensity of your new life or career. You get to design the support system that works for you.

To create an effective support system and structure for your life, you'll need to build a network of people who you trust and respect the most. These will be like your new teammates, coaches, strength trainers, agents, etc., and they will help you achieve your big life goals. Here are some tips to get the ball rolling:

❖ Pick three people to be your positive support system (training partners); share your plan/goal with them and request that they check in on you regularly. You may offer to do the same for them or give them a small gift for supporting you.

❖ Join the Transition... What Now? community at transitionwhatnow.com

❖ Get the media on your side. Use social media or write an article about the goals you are setting out to achieve, and submit it to a magazine, online publication, or your local newspaper.

❖ Be a Big Brother or Big Sister (bbbs.org) and teach a portion of this book to him or her. Make a plan to do this together; modify and apply the method to their life goals. Commit to each other.

❖ Find a teammate or form a team, and complete this book together; set up a structure with weekly calls or meetings to support each other.

❖ Get booked on a talk show for your efforts in what you are creating in your life.

❖ Start a blog, Pinterest, Vlog, podcast, YouTube channel or other medium discussing what you're doing.

❖ Speak to local schools or clubs and share your story.

❖ Set up email support with friends all over the world.

❖ Talk to a trusted religious/spiritual source.

❖ Join or form a life/community group.

❖ Form a meet-up on meetup.com

❖ Post to a social network and ask for support.

❖ Get a personal coach (life, spiritual, business or health).

❖ Put something at stake for your goal (reward / consequence) and find someone to hold you accountable.

There are many ways to create a support system. Design your own, using whatever methods work for you. This is crucial to your success. When you put yourself out there publicly and demand results and action from yourself, you will achieve your goals. Don't attempt to take this on by yourself. Imagine playing your sport with zero support. No coach, no team, no fans, no cheering, no retweets, no likes, no endorsements, nothing at stake, no encouragement. Your career wouldn't be as fulfilling, as joyous, as honorable, as rich, or as successful . . . would it?

Your goal is to surround yourself with more support than you know what to do with. Accountability and encouragement are huge players.

The finest gift you can give anyone is encouragement. Yet, almost no one gets the encouragement they need to grow to their full potential. If everyone received the encouragement they need to grow, the genius in most everyone would blossom and the world would produce abundance beyond their wildest dreams. –Sidney Madwed

With support you will come to realize that the discomfort of the stretch is temporary, while the gain is forever. As a former gymnast, I don't recommend having someone push your hips to the floor in a middle split until you cry, but I do recommend applying some pressure, getting a good stretch, and allowing your muscles to relax/expand.structure Get supple, get in action, and get support!

Personal Support Structure (PSS):

_____

_____

_____

_____

_____

_____

Share Opp- @transitionwhatnow post what support structure you have set up that will help you stay committed to your Five Secrets and #boundtoglory.

- ★ Give yourself 2 points for creating a Personal Support Structure._____
- ★ Give yourself 2 points for working the Personal Support Structure._____

Life's goal is not to die and leave a beautiful corpse, but rather to slide into the grave sideways shouting...Wow! WHAT A RIDE! – Hunter S. Thompson

Celebrity Interview: Svetlana Boguinskaia

Janae– I am here with Svetlana Boguinskaia, who has won 5 Olympic medals and 5 World gold medals and 9 European golds. You are currently one of the few gymnasts to ever compete in three Olympic Games. You are an icon in the gymnastics world known as the Belarusian Swan. I am thrilled to have you here today, to answer some questions and share your story, so thank you very much for being here with me. One thing I wanted to start with, different than most athletes I have interviewed who have grown up and trained in America is that you grew up in the Soviet Union so I wanted to have you share a little bit about what it was like to train in the Soviet Union which is now Belarus.

Svetlana– What it was like to train in former Soviet Union and now Belarus growing up? Well that is a good question. I didn't know any difference between my country and any others because this is the only country I grew up with. I was born in this part of the country to do gymnastics at age six. It was very exciting from the beginning. I really fell in love with the sport because I was naturally talented and gifted in gymnastics. And in sport area but in that particular sport. I think my coach saw potential but I guess she couldn't show it because she didn't want to show a favorite child from the group of gymnasts. That group was 30 from the beginning.

Then after three months validation, what happens in my country when you start to do gymnastics, you have 30 kids, just about 30 kids from age five and a half to six and a half (you're not allowed to send any younger than that because the coaches think you are not old enough to understand and follow instructions– you just want to play around) from the get go, they want you to give their attention and repeat cues and do everything you need to do to become a great gymnast. It is like a machine. They produce great athletes from the beginning.

So from that 30 kids for three months you only do conditioning and ballet. And then they evaluate you– your physical, how strong you are. By your conditioning test, from that 30 kids only 10 can stay. So I ended up in this group of 10 girls. Where I was training in the beginning once a week training three hours a day. Then it became three days a week three hours a day. Then five days a week for four to five hours a day. It was lots of fun and I really like that but I didn't know any different.

Now as growing up and living in America, I understand how much fun kids have here. I think we did have fun but it was different fun. We did play games but it was definitely the games we had to work hard without even realizing. "Who could do 100 leg lifts faster?" They would get a sticker. "Who can do 100 push ups the best?" So it was the games, but it was different kind of games then they have here. I really enjoy my childhood growing up and doing gymnastics in my country.

Janae- *Following retirement what were the first few years like for you after retiring from competitive gymnastics?*

Svetlana- *What are the first few years for me like after retiring from gymnastics? Well, I did retire a few times. My first time I retired after '92 Olympics I was 19. That was probably the hardest retirement. That's what made me come back to gymnastics. Because I really didn't know what to do with myself. Coming home from the '92 Olympics I didn't really get any support from the Belarusian Federation. They did give me flowers and a "Thank you for representing our country competing for Russia and Belarus as well. If you need to get a job as coach we can help you." I didn't really need any help in a coaching job for that matter.*

All of your life people did things for you. Everybody thought you were special and they took care of you. All of a sudden you are alone. They did booking for you. They book your airline tickets and hotel, etc. I just didn't know how to do all of those basic things. I probably should have but everybody did things for me so I didn't really have to know. I did some travel on tours in Europe and United States as well. From twelve months you take maybe three months traveling and have maybe nine months to do nothing. I did finish college so I didn't really have much to do. Except just go out and partying, I was good but also I really didn't have a place as a job to do. I didn't want it at the time because I'm still trying to find myself.

I decided to take a job to come to United States and work with Woodward camp. They were the ones who invited me here at age 20 and I decided to stay here because I love this country. Then I tried to find myself here in the States as well. Learning the language, and crying. I didn't really like it cause I couldn't speak to anybody. It was hard times. I knew I would be okay in the day time and I would cry in my pillow at night because I thought that I was stupid. I couldn't talk to anybody because I was afraid to make any mistakes in a foreign language and that those people would make fun of me. You know I had different issues I have to go through. Then I got the opportunity to meet Bela at a USGTC camp in Boston. And he said, "Why don't you come back from your retirement? It will be in Atlanta '96 and you have two and a half years to go for that." He started a group of girls including Kim Zmeskal and upcoming Dominique Moceanu and Betty Okino who's coming out of retirement to try to make it to the team for the '96 Olympics.

The invitation... I thought to myself, "Why didn't I try to go back to gymnastics because it's what gave me my life it's what I enjoy?" I enjoyed doing gymnastics. Just enjoyed having a place where I belong somewhere. To a Belarusian team, to a Russian team to whatever team it was. I choose to come back to the sport. Then after when I retired after '96 Olympics it was a little bit different because I was already in America. I already learned the language. Life is easier. I learned how to communicate, how to work in a gym, how to organize things. And being on tours you learn, you see people doing things, anything. I thought, "My gosh I can do the same thing." I travel to different camps, I thought, "Why don't I try to do my camp and see what's going to happen from that?" Because I can give so much. It was a much easier transition to retirement.

Janae– Yes. That second retirement was much easier. Is there anything you could think of during those first years that would have made transition easier?

Svetlana– I think if I would have a person or somebody to talk to– to educate. What do you do after you come from the Olympic gold to the real world? Where you don't have any other talents? You are on top of the world and then where do you go from there? I think the only choices is the way down and to find yourself. So if I were to have a person who I can talk to and could give me what to do how to start my life that would be very helpful.

Janae– What can coaches do to better prepare athletes for retirement?

Svetlana– What can coaches do to better prepare for retirement? I think they probably should talk to them more, especially when you're getting a little bit older getting to 16 to 17 year olds. Just tell them. They have a life and gymnastics is gymnastics. That's what I'm telling the kids. Gymnastics is hard wait till you're retired and go into the real world. Life is not going to get any easier. This is hard day after day and you have to be up for the challenge. If coaches could tell us that too, you know, maybe better prepare us. To tell us gymnastics is one thing and if you think it's hard wait until you see what's going to happen because challenges is a day to day challenge. You have to go to interview you have to get a job. You have to get a job and you have to keep a job. And things like that. I think coaches should just talk to us more about those things.

Janae- So gymnastics was one of the biggest blessings in my life as it was yours. And it is such a unique and powerful sport. However I was speaking with a former elite gymnast the other day and she had trained with a lot of the Olympians, her family was uprooted to train with the best in Pennsylvania. She broke her back and never became an Olympian. She did do gymnastics in college at a smaller school. She has graduated from college, owned her own gym, stayed involved with the sport- coaching. She has been around the sport for 28 years. She is really struggling. She stays involved in the sport because she is scared to leave it. It is all she knows. As you said it wasn't that she wasn't really talented. She's burned out, she has struggles with issues such as; identity, self image, control, feeling purposeless. What I feel, is that this woman is not alone. Many athletes of the past who even after years of retirement are still in the sport are still struggling. What do you think causes these issues later in life? And what do you think can be done to help prevent this?

Svetlana- Hmm. Why do we see lots of gymnasts struggle? I tell myself you really shouldn't be living in the past, you have to look in the future. I never really think anymore that I won so many medals. I really don't talk about it much to the people I meet, they don't even know who I am just think I'm an all around girl. I am just trying to not even talk about that because I think it was in the past and now I have to do something in the future. I have to do something right now. Help me go through the day because what can I do about it today to make it better for tomorrow?

Instead of what have I done in the past they can make me to a better life in the future. Really I shouldn't be thinking about that. So I think maybe people like you who can teach us. Or teach just a group of people who are coming from a professional sport.

Well, not even a professional sport but young athletes who are retiring early to have more people like you to talk to us about that psychology or I'm not sure ...mentor just give us advice in the future life. Because it is really hard and I do think about it a lot, a lot, what is my purpose in life? Yes I was so good in something. It is hard and it's depressing and sometimes I get into depressions about that. Maybe once a year I have this phase for you know one or two a days where I just want to lay in my bed and cry and cry and cry because I'm thinking what is my purpose in life now?

Janae– *Yes, then again it is so tough because you have seen and been in such a winning position when you are winning Olympic gold medals...*

Svetlana– *Yes. So it is really not easy and I'm sure I am NOT the only one. I am sure there probably every athlete who is been there maybe almost made it even regular athletes, level 10 gymnast, college athletes, probably struggle. We really need to make something together to educate and talk about it to have some kind of flyer distribution or a book...a book about that. That wouldn't be a bad idea!*

Janae– *Anything else you would like to share about your experience in gymnastics or anything else you would like to add?*

Svetlana– *Hmmm. I would like to add gymnastics was my favorite sport that I think, well that is the reason is my favorite, because I was good at it. It gave me so much in life. Especially my friends. It is not an easy sport at times it was hard. I wanted to quit pretty much every single day because I didn't understand what am I doing? Day to day basis working hard and it was physical work. But definitely hard work pays off.*

So tell the young girls to work hard in the gym or in the skill area or other place in whatever you do in life. If you work hard, you get results in the end. So don't give up, keep working hard and the end result will be positive.

Janae- *Beautiful.*

UPDATE:

International Hall of Fame Inductee

Svetlana continues to lead Olympia Gymnastics Camps (www.ocgcamp.com) and appearances worldwide at a variety of events.

Married– with a son and a daughter.

Family owned– Mazzei's Gourmet Pizza

Interview Takeaway:

_____

_____

_____

_____

_____

_____

_____

_____

_____

_____

_____

Celebrity Interview: Buddy Biancalana

Janae– *I am thrilled to introduce an incredibly successful baseball player that has produced wild success on and off field with an eleven year professional baseball career. He starred in the 1985 world series and had the highest number of votes for MVP for any position player. He has appeared on TV shows such as David Letterman and the Today show. Thank you for being here Buddy Biancalana.*

Buddy– *You're welcome. Nice to be here.*

Janae– *So, to get started, I just wanted to also mention that I know you do a lot of work with current players and you have a web business called peak performance baseball. Can you tell me a little about that and what you have going on there.*

Buddy– *Sure. It all stems from my zone experience playing for my 1985 World Series ring. I had a level of concentration I have never hit before to the point where I felt like I could do no wrong. After that time, my life kind of tumbled a little bit. I went through divorce, I had injuries and went through depression, anxiety. That experience of playing the series of '85. Having that peak performance in knowing if we have that experience once, we can usually experience it many times if not on a daily basis of living in the zone. It was through that experience and the tough times to follow that umm really sent me on a search for basically more awareness and ways that I can feel the way I felt in that seven game World Series where my mind was very still and very very focused. And consequently have developed my peak performance baseball program that I utilize, mainly I work with* *hitters. That is my real passion; teaching hitters and utilizing peak performance technique that I do to enhance their ability to expedite development but certainly effective for all athletes.*

Janae– Got it. Thank you. So being one of America's top athletes who did reach the top of your game as 1985 World Series champion. Is there a moment that you decided you weren't going to be a baseball player anymore and how did you make that decision?

Buddy– Well I had a back injury and I had neck problems and the game just wasn't fun. Because of the physical injuries. It was certainly affecting me mentally to the point where it wasn't fun at all to go to the park and play. When there are blocks in your physiology...life is challenging enough. When there are energetic blocks then it really becomes difficult to the point where I just felt like and thought, well, the doctors wouldn't release me to play. But I was mentally really burnt out with the game. And the problem with me at the time was I just wasn't strong enough. My whole being was so tied to baseball. You know my self worth was determined by how I played. If I played well I felt good If I played poorly I didn't feel good. You know it is very codependent. Certainly those times I would not trade.

Those struggles certainly got me to the point where I am now. Life is really cool. Once you kind of figure out how life works and start to flow with it a little bit instead of swimming upstream, it becomes interesting and really exciting. Even in the times that are challenging you know I now can sit back and witness those events and know that these things are just kind of moving me on to the next things where I am supposed to be headed. And I certainly don't have the ups and down emotionally. Not that it is always comfortable. But it is really fun and exciting to witness life's ebb and flow.

Janae– Yeah. I think myself as an athlete and the athletes I have spoken to can really relate to what you said in the beginning with the esteem and confidence related to performance. And I think the resistance to how we perform that can knock us off our game and not going with the ebb and flow of how it happens. That is definitely something I hear a lot about.

Buddy– Right. And we have all heard of the 'fear of failure.' But I have experienced that 'fear of success.' Which is really cumbersome when you fearing either direction. You know you have to walk down this thin white line and if I got too good then I felt like "Oh everyone is expecting of me." And if I played poorly I would say "Geeze, I could get released or traded." Whatever it is I have got to play better just this back and forth and there was discomfort...really no matter how I was playing. Sure I was happier when I was playing well but there was a level of discomfort that came upon me after a certain time of playing well...boy it was really crummy. But again I wouldn't trade it. I wouldn't trade the experiences for what it has taught me.

Janae– 100% of athletes face career termination. You had to make that transition from baseball player to life beyond sport. What was that transition out of baseball like for you and what happened?

Buddy– Well it was very difficult. I think it depends on the state of the athlete. You know. I had physical injury that affected me mentally and emotionally. I had emotional and mental... my mindset wasn't what it should be I had unresolved emotional issues. So, one affects the other to the extent that an athlete is affected by any one of those three areas emotional, mental, or physical. Their experience is certainly going to be a little different. In my case I then became aware I had some severe neck injuries that I think stem back to as early as baby when I fell of a changing table. The fact that I stopped crying everyone thought I was ok. We all know that as we get older some of our old injuries can creep up. I believe that has a great deal to do with the fear that I experience playing the game, fear of failure, the whole level of confidence and self esteem that I had. I know it affected me mentally and how I slept. My whole nervous system was in disarray.

That being said, that is going to affect every aspect of our life. Every aspect of our life is affected by every other aspect of our life. It is a matter of getting all those areas in harmony and congruency. As far as the transition, it wasn't easy. Certainly I was a high school grad who passed on college to accept a big contract. I was the number one draft pick of the Kansas City Royals in 1978. I had every intention to go to college. Yet my dream staring me in the face and I accepted the offer from KC and signed and began my professional career at age 18. And baseball was my life from the time I was 9. I was from a very well educated family. So I had that going for me so I felt like I could always communicate well. I felt like I had a lot going for me despite not having the college education. But the transition you know I felt leaving baseball. I always admired a guy like Bryant Gumbel who was so successful in sports broadcasting and went off and did other areas of life and extended his broadcasting career beyond sports. I felt like I wanted to be more than just a quote "jock" and I got into commercial real estate. And wasn't real successful. Again my physical health is not good at all, it is such a challenge. The stress of all of that caused a lot of disruption in my marriage so we ended up splitting up and divorcing. Which is not uncommon for athletes who are certainly searching for themselves. After their career is over after that huge part of them is taken away. So that all came about and then not knowing where I belonged in the world. Being able to search was awesome. It was great. By that time I was very confused and in a lot of pain, depression, anxiety, physical pain, emotional pain certainly. I sought out a lot of help. I had great mentors. There is tremendous help. There is no need for anyone to suffer in this world. You can be in pain and you can feel the pain but as far as suffering emotionally and mentally there is so much help available that I believe that unless there is just severe brain damage I really feel that you can really be helped and go on to live a really enjoyable life and really get in the flow of life and understand how the universal energy works. How God works. And it is a beautiful process.

Janae- When you were leaving baseball what do you feel like you did really well and were successful at in your transition?

Buddy- Seeking the help to get me on a path where I have a lot of confidence. I did not sit back and turn to things that were unhealthy for me – you know alcohol, drugs or sex. Whatever other addictions people can turn to. I really sat in the discomfort. Which is what I think is the key. I felt the discomfort. Which for me is really really important for someone to do instead of altering and trying to get out of that pain that people feel.

Janae- Go straight through it right?

Buddy- You gotta go into it. I think as scary as it can be or some people you have to go to the real dark hole of your soul. When you do there is this tremendous brightness and light on the other side of that darkness. It is really a cool thing to do.

Janae- *What was the most challenging aspect of retirement? Which you may have already touched on some.*

Buddy- *Yeah. I would have to say- what was causing what? What was causing the pain that I felt? The physical, the emotional pain that I felt. The hardest thing is to discern what is physical, what is emotional... and for so many people in this environment it is so difficult because of all the toxicity of the whole environment. The emotional toxicity. The toxicity we get from foods we eat. Living in this world nowadays, especially in this country is a tremendous challenge to be healthy and feel great. I am not sure how many people do. Certainly that is my challenge and there is no reason why people can't be very successful and be very wealthy. But...to be very very whole, and at peace, and earning money for all of the right reasons and spending it on causes and things that are going to benefit mankind. That is different.*

Janae- *What has been helpful for you in transition?*

Buddy- *To have all this knowledge and maturity. I think for me what would have been helpful is that coaches saying this is what we are going to do. Not be taken to the American obsession to be more successful. It's not just going to the batting cage everyday, outfield or in grounding balls certainly there is going to be plenty of that. We are going to address all of these other areas on a regular basis. With the intention to strengthen all these areas and find out where we are missing the boat in one area and how is affecting another area of life which is obviously also affecting our performance on the baseball field. Once we are able to do that then we are going to have the best darn baseball players in an era. We have gone through an era where performance enhancement is a huge term. It's so big people have turned to steroids to enhance performance. Well obviously* steroids work but they are not good, they are very detrimental to the body; a lot of people are paying the price for it. Does that mean we won't hit 70 home runs again? I don't know. I am not that smart but I do know they're going to have more form, more consistency. They are going to be able to digest more quickly. They will play with more confidence, will be happier, more energetic and more successful. They are going to be better for the public- contributing more to society. As one becomes more aware and feeling better about themselves, they will be able to give to more people. This great game of baseball will get better and better and better.

Janae- What advice Buddy do you have for athletes today who are facing the challenge of leaving your sport?

Buddy- To take time and grieve over the loss. Take time to themselves in solitude. And really feel the loss of not having a sport, that appeal to perform on. If you are not dealing with the emotional feelings they will bottle up and really create havoc and cause you from moving forward. Your feelings are essential. Quieting the mind is essential. Pythagoras the philosopher back in the 1400's said, the head of all man's problems come from not quieting the mind on a regular basis. We can get too busy in life and we don't take the time to take stock and seek answers, which they are always there. People can get off course. So those two things I would recommend for any athlete facing closure in sport.

Janae- In your experience with athletes and baseball players that you have come across what have you seen them struggle from in retirement.

Buddy- Well- divorce is common, some have turned to drugs

and alcohol to deal with struggles as well. Not having an education and all of those things are areas that athletes struggle with. There are moments we feel sorry for ourselves, but they are all moments that my belief is we reach our own path in life and that goes way beyond what is seen with the naked eye. Or what all five senses can detect. There's no reason to feel sorry. Ask for help and guidance. And certainly that is what I try and do when I see somebody in need. Sometimes they are just not open to it which is okay because they need to be at a point of their evolutionary path. Anything more than a suggestion is interfering with somebody's journey getting back to what I said earlier everybody has a right to their own journey. People and events are put into our life and we need to be there. We don't want to force ourselves on anybody.

Janae- One of the areas I work with athletes on is creating a life beyond sport that can exceed the rewards and glory of being an athlete. Many of the athletes that I speak with constantly live their life looking back in the rear view mirror seeing their life can never get better than that feeling. What would you recommend for these athletes that cannot even see the possibility of a better life beyond sport for themselves?

Buddy- Well I believe that everything we do in life we are doing to achieve greater peace of mind and we are looking to change how we feel. We are looking for greater highs. The high is created internally okay so an athlete that hit a grand slam in the bottom of the ninth inning in game seven in the World Series, you know, that... that feeling experience I try to explain to him... that is a feeling that is your own feeling. It is an external experience that created that feeling, but your physiology experiences it. It's a reaction to an action. You know most of them can understand that. And know that yes it was an external *event that triggered it but you are the one who chose the reaction. You have control over your reaction.*

Certainly there are outside influences that cause feelings but the power and the peace of mind can come often from within and that is what I would advise an athlete. Those highs you experienced playing, you can experience within your own being. Utilize that to contribute to society and to help others and whatever purpose you're here to fulfill besides hitting a grand slam in the ninth inning of the game seven of the World Series. You will come to that, seek and you shall find. That is a true statement. I know it to be. If you just keep seeking and seeking, you will find. And people are seeking through alcohol and other forms of things that take them further away from feeling that experience and feeling that great high that is achievable in their own being, it is available naturally.

Janae- So you are saying that there is that grand slam in the ninth inning of the World Series... in life?

Buddy- Absolutely! It lasts for life. There is no question about it. And that is what I believe we are all here for. To achieve that experience. Sport is a great playground for seeking fulfillment beyond successful performance because you are going to fail so many times that it is a constant challenge. How would you keep yourself upbeat? Just like today, we have lost two in a row and I'm thinking "What are we going to do?" And I love it, I love it because if we just kept winning and winning and winning it's nice, but there is no challenge. So I made my list, ok here is what we are going to hit on; the player's we are going to work with right now. This player needs urgent help...and so on. That is great. It is the seeking –the great thing about life it is the journey not the destination. If we keep waiting for the destination, it is not going to be fulfilled. Home run happens, you get the exhilaration, now what? You know, we won game seven, what now?

Janae– I know there are many athletes beyond baseball even, who can hear this and really grab something for themselves.

Buddy– Well thank you for all you are doing. You are doing some fabulous fabulous stuff and I know you are going to touch many many people.

Janae– Thank you.

UPDATE:

*Buddy– The website is **pmpmsports.com**. I have taught The Fluid Motion Factor to athletes in seven professional and fourteen amateur sports. The program is endorsed by world renowned golf instructor, David Leadbetter.*

Interview Takeaway:

_____

_____

_____

_____

_____

_____

_____

_____

College Interview: Maria

(Former Penn State University Gymnast, current work from home, full-time mother of three)

Janae- What doesn't work about your life after sport? What's missing?

Maria- It is hard to stay constantly motivated to workout and do it for myself. I always had something to work for or I had to be in shape. So as far as that goes, that has been difficult. I do miss having something to work for, the competitions and daily goals and motivation of working towards those goals. I miss the camaraderie of a team and working together.

Janae- Have you discovered a new dream that has you jumping out of bed each morning? Or are you surviving? Although I do know that even as a gymnast, we did not jump out of bed for 6:30 morning lifting!

Maria- Ha! I haven't had anything such as a new dream thus far...nothing that has jumped out of me.

FOLLOW UP:

Janae- Here we are nearly 10 years later. What have you accomplished in this time?

Maria- Wow, hard to believe it's been that long! I would have to say my biggest accomplishment has been becoming a mom to a beautiful girl, Abigail, precious little boy Wesley and are also blessed to be expecting our third little one in November. I continue to be fulfilled by my husband and marriage of eight years.

Janae– How has your experience as an athlete propelled your future?

Maria– I would say that the qualities that are developed as an athlete serve you well for life after sport. I have noticed the parallel a lot just in parenting. I find myself comparing my schedule to my time as an athlete; being able to multitask, time management skills, determination to get everything done, being organized, wanting your kids to work hard and strive for set goals. I think that the skills I learned will always be able to benefit me personally and also to help me guide my kids as they head down their own paths.

Janae– What was the most challenging point of your life post retirement from sport?

Maria– I read my previous responses about what was missing from life after sport. All of what I previously stated was true, but at that time I was not ready to physically work out and was not really self-motivated to get to a gym. I would say I was pretty burned out and mostly, my body was ready for a break! However, probably about five years later (six months after giving birth to my son), I developed that passion and drive all over again simply from attending one bootcamp style class that my "mommy friend" was attending. She said, "Maria, if I can do it, you sure can!" I went one time and was hooked. It was the ONLY thing that gave me the same motivation and drive to work hard and get back in shape that I had felt as an athlete. I became hooked again and not only was I able to lose about 25 pounds of baby weight, but was able to get into the best shape I had been in since being an athlete. The personal trainer held me accountable and motivated me to want to improve and work hard. It was a great feeling! I never realized how much I had missed that feeling of working hard, teamwork (as there were a bunch of us in this class), and even aching muscles! I had that competitive fire re-lit inside of me and loved doing something just for ME again.

Janae- For me, the challenges in transition from sport diminished when I became less and less able physically to compete at a high level, having a family and finding my purpose. What was that point of acceptance and moving forward for you?

Maria- I agree with you that, it becomes easier once you have family and kids, but as I stated above, it was so helpful to also realize that I needed to make working out and taking care of me a priority because I realized how much it affected me and my family in a positive way!

Janae- What is your advice for athletes transitioning out of sport today who are not yet at a stage of acceptance?

Maria- I would just say that it is hard to figure out your identity as a person outside of being an athlete. I think to this day, in your head, you still see yourself in that way at times. I think it was helpful to me when I started a family to help me see the big picture of life. And that your world and focus turns to something else, which at the time will be so important and fulfilling to you! I was able to have much better perspective and realize that being an athlete had such a tremendous impact on me growing up and the person that I am today, but I am NOT that person now. You *find new things that identify you and make you happy and you take with you all the things you learned from being an athlete.*

Janae- *Thank you Maria.*

Interview Takeaway:

_____

_____

_____

_____

_____

_____

_____

_____

_____

_____

Congratulations!

You have completed the Five Secrets!

Secret 1: Identity
Secret 2: Vision
Secret 3: Foundation
Secret 4: Plan
Secret 5: Structure and Support

You have now completed the work!

You have done a lot of work (both passive and active), now it's time to assess your progress.

Chapter Nine

End Assessment

1. How inspired are you about your life beyond sport now? (0 is not at all, 10 is you are jumping out of your skin) Explain:

_____

_____

_____

_____

_____

_____

2. Rate your ability to exist in this world without your sport defining you. (0 is I am completely defined by my sport, 10 is my relationship to my sport is healthy) Explain:

_____

_____

_____

_____

_____

3. How confident are you in your ability to win in life overall beyond sport, for example: financially, relationally, emotionally, physically, and professionally? (0 is not confident at all, 10 is extremely confident)

_____

_____

_____

_____

4. Do you feel supported with a clear direction and plan for your life beyond sport? (0 is I feel completely lost, 10 is completely supported and clear) Explain:

_____

_____

_____

_____

_____

5. Did your list of three results you would like to accomplish in your life change? Are you more confident in achieving these results now? Explain:

_____

_____

_____

_____

_____

6. Does your # 1 thing that stopped you from achieving those results still get in your way? Explain:

_____

_____

_____

_____

_____

7. Is your biggest challenge in life now non existent or less of a road block and more of a hurdle you can jump over?

Explain:

_____

_____

_____

_____

_____

_____

8. Did you accomplish your one goal for this book? Why or why not?

_____

_____

_____

_____

_____

_____

Share Opp- @transitionwhatnow post whether you did or did not accomplish your one goal from this book and why and #unstoppable.

Now add up your total points here._____ out of 25. You may want to do the math twice.

23-25: GOLD - Congratulations! You have done what it takes to win at retiring from sport. You are on your way to big wins—watch out world!

21-22: SILVER - Great work! You have launched your journey and are set up to win! Great things will come from you.

18-20: BRONZE - You are well ahead of the game. Go get 'em. Feel free to revisit the book again. The world is your oyster.

17 or below: PARTICIPANT – As they say, 80% of success is just showing up. You are definitely on your way. You can do it. Take a few months off and then revisit the book.

I would love to hear your feedback on your journey through this book at: Transitionwhatnow.com

Chapter Ten

Trust Your Training

Congratulations on suiting up and getting back into the game of life. If you are struggling, know it is completely normal and expected. Do not give up on life, dreams, marriage, healing, faith, people, finances, etc. Use this workbook and get the support you need to move through life healthfully. You are being refined, and the process can be uncomfortable. Remember that the goal of this book is not to omit the work but to make it easier, keeping in mind, the best is yet to come! Joy is yours for the taking. Don't allow life's distractions/struggles to bog you down and keep you from living. You are unique, you are needed! The momentum you have created will allow you to go forth and conquer. If you need additional accountability or support, visit: transitionwhatnow.com.

Feel free to put this book down for a bit, practice your new tools in life. Then come back and do it again at a later date for more refining. Use this as a reference, not just a one time shot. You will find that different phases of your retirement you have different experiences that may warrant a refresher of this book. It will also be rewarding later in life, to review notes from previous times you worked through the Five Secrets.

You have worked so hard through the Five Secrets. You have sacrificed so much in the sports arena and now in the life arena. Watch the following video and/or read the lyrics. End with a perspective of all that you have sacrificed and gained.

Video Assignment: "Why Do We Fall—Motivational Video."
YouTube link (original): http://youtu.be/mgmVOuLgFB0

Read the lyrics, let them resonate, motivate you, and put your sacrifice into perspective:

Why Do We Fall - Motivational Video Script:

Let me tell you something you already know.
The world ain't all sunshine and rainbows.
It's a very mean and nasty place and I don't care how tough you are, it will beat you to your knees and keep you there permanently if you let it.
You, me or nobody, is gonna hit as hard as life. But it ain't about how hard ya hit.
It's about how hard you can get hit and keep moving forward. How much you can take, and keep moving forward. That's how winning is done!
Pain is temporary. It may last for a minute, or an hour, or a day, or even a year. But eventually, it will subside and something else will take its place. If I quit, however, it will last forever.
The margin for error is so small, I mean,
one-half a step too late, or too early, and you don't quite make it.
One half-second too slow or too fast, you don't quite catch it.
The inches we need are everywhere around us. They're in every break of the game, every minute, every second.
You got a dream, you gotta protect it. People can't do somethin' themselves, they wanna tell you you can't do it.
If you want somethin', go get it. Period.
Don't be afraid to fail.

You can't always win, but don't be afraid of making decisions.

You have to believe that something different can happen.

"He who says he can, and he who says he can't, are both usually right." (Henry Ford)

Now most of you say you want to be successful, but you don't want it bad, you just "kinda" want it.

You don't want it badder than you wanna party.

You don't want it as much as you want to be cool.

Most of you don't want success as much as you want to sleep!

Our deepest fear is not that we are inadequate.

Our deepest fear is that we are powerful beyond measure.

It is our light, not our darkness that most frightens us.

You have to dig deep down, dig deep down, and ask yourselves, who do you want to be?

Figuring out for yourselves what makes you happy

no matter how crazy it may sound to other people.

Make a choice, right? You just decide

what it's gonna be, who you're gonna be, how you're gonna do it. Just decide.

Why not, why can't I be the MVP of the league? Why can't I be the best player in the league? I don't see why. Why? Why can't I do that?

What did you say to the kid? It ain't about how hard you hit.

It's about how hard you can get hit and keep moving forward.

How much you can take, and keep moving forward.

Get up!

Get up!

Get up, and don't ever give up.

We can stay here, get the sh#* kicked out of us

OR

We can fight our way back, into the light. We can climb, out of hell.

One inch at a time.

To be able at any moment to sacrifice what you are for what you will become.

Most of you won't be successful because when you're studying, and you get tired, you quit.

"I don't do well in math," you're right! You ain't never studied.

"I'm not good at writing," 'cause you have never written before!

Talent you have naturally. Skill is only developed by hours and hours and hours of beating on your craft.

If you're not making someone else's life better, then you're wasting your time.

Don't cry to give up, cry to keep going.

Don't cry to quit! You already in pain, you already hurt. Get a reward for it.

Now if you know what you're worth, then go ahead and get what you're worth, but you gotta be willing to take the hit and

not point fingers saying you ain't where you wanna be because of him or her or anybody.

Cowards do that and that ain't you!

You're better than that!

Because everyday is a new day. Every moment is a new moment!

So now you gotta go out and show them that I'm a different creature. Now!

I'ma show you how great I am!

In the 17th chapter of Luke it is written, "The Kingdom of God is within man." Not one man nor a group of men, but

in all men. In you! You, the people, have the power:
the power to create machines, the power to create
happiness.
You, the people, have the power to make this life free and
beautiful, to make this life a wonderful adventure. Now,
what are you gonna do?
Because limits, like fears, are often just an illusion.

That is one motivational speech!

This is how hard you fought for your athletic career, now you will fight this hard for life beyond athletics. You fall, you get up, you are on purpose in this wonderful adventure. On the field, off the field, same thing. Get up and don't give up!

As Thoreau says, *Go confidently in the direction of your dreams. Live the life you've imagined!*

Your best is yet to come!

Reflections on Journey

Appendix

Books that shaped my journey:

- *What to Say When You Talk to Yourself.* Shad Helmstetter
- *The Magic of Thinking Big.* David J, Schwartz
- *Season of Life.* Jeffrey Marx
- *Think and Grow Rich.* Napoleon Hill
- *How to Play the Game of Your Life* - a guide to success in sports- and life. George A. Selleck, PhD.
- *Blink.* Malcolm Gladwell
- *The Tipping Point.* Malcolm Gladwell
- *Switch on Your Brain.* Dr. Caroline Leaf
- *The Good Life.* Charles Colson
- *The Unseen Essential.* James P. Gills, M.D.
- *Love Does.* Bob Goff
- *SHAPE – Finding and Fulfilling your God Given Purpose.* Erik Rees
- *The 7 Habits of Highly Effective People.* Stephen R. Covey
- *Platform- Get Noticed in a Noisy World.* Michael Hyatt
- *Book Yourself Solid.* Michael Port
- *The 4 Hour Work Week.* Timothy Ferriss

Notes & Citations

Chapter Two

1. Baillie, P. H. F., & Danish, S. J. Understanding the career transition of athletes. Sport Psychologist, 1992. P77-98.
2. Reuttgers, Ken. Gamesover.org. Retrieved June 2006. (Site no longer available).
3. Hayman and Andersen. Journal Of Excellence. Issue #13. 2009 (McKnight et al).
4. Ferriss, Timothy. The 4-Hour Workweek: Escape 9-5, Live Anywhere, and Join the New Rich. Crown Publishing Group, 2007. P21.
5. Marquette, Terra. Study: Retired Athletes Struggle With Loss Of Sports Culture, Finding New Identity. Happiness, Psychological, Sports. February 28, 2018.
6. Colson, Charles. The Good Life - Seeking Purpose, Meaning and Truth in Your Life. Carol Stream, Tyndale, 2006.
7. Millman, Dan. Interview. 2005.
8. www.Dictionary.com. Retrieved July, 2005

Chapter Four

9. Baillie, P. H. F., & Danish, S. J. Understanding the career transition of athletes. Sport Psychologist, 1992. P77-98.

10. Baillie, P. H. F., & Danish, S. J. Understanding the career transition of athletes. Sport Psychologist, 1992. P77-98.
11. Hayman and Andersen. Journal Of Excellence. Issue #13. 2009 (McKnight et al). p63.
12. "I AM - The shift is about to hit the fan." www.Iamthedoc.com. Dir. Tom Shadyac. Flying Eye Productions. 2010.
13. Rees, Erik. S.H.A.P.E. - Finding and Fulfilling Your Unique Purpose in Life. Grand Rapids: Zondervan, 2008.

Chapter Five

14. Matthews, Gail, Ph.D., Dominican University. Gail Matthews Written Goal Study Dominican University. Retrieved February 12, 2014.

Chapter Six

15. www.Dictionary.com. Retrieved July, 2005.
16. Strydom, MK. Healing Begins With Sanctification of the Heart. Harare, Zimbabwe. PrintWorks, 2013. 4th Edition. P7
17. Strydom, MK. Healing Begins With Sanctification of the Heart. Harare, Zimbabwe. PrintWorks, 2013. 4th Edition. P23

Chapter Seven

18. Arnold, Alison, Ph. D. The Athlete Warrior: Creating an Unshakable Mind. www.headgamesworld.com. P75.

19. www.astd.org. America Society of Training and Development. Retrieved 2005.

20. http://www.prweb.com/releases/2010/04/prweb3825384.htm?PID=4003003 "New Leadership IQ Paper Asks, Are SMART Goals Dumb?" Murphy, Mark. Retrieved February 6, 2014.

21. Ferriss, Timothy. The 4-Hour Workweek: Escape 9-5, Live Anywhere, and Join the New Rich. Crown Publishing Group, 2007. p43, 46.

Chapter Ten

22. You Tube: Why Do We Fall- Motivational Video: http://youtu.be/mgmVOuLgFBo. July, 2014.

Celebrity Interviews: 2005/6 & 2013

1. Biancalana, Buddy. Ali, Janae W. 2005 & 2013.
2. Boguinskaia, Svetlana. Ali, Janae W. 2005.
3. Ehrmann, Joe. Ali, Janae W. 2005.
4. Retton, Mary Lou. Ali, Janae W. 2006 & 2013.
5. Millman, Dan. Ali, Janae W. 2005 & 2018.
6. McCoy, Kerry. Ali, Janae W. 2006 & 2013.
7. Tedder, Amy. Ali, Janae W. 2006 & 2013.

College Interviews: 2005/6 & 2013 (Last names omitted)

1. Ellen. Ali, Janae W. 2006 & 2013.
2. Brent. Ali, Janae W. 2006.
3. Carey. Ali, Janae W. 2006 & 2013.
4. Chris. Ali, Janae W. 2006.
5. Maria. Ali, Janae W. 2006 & 2013.
6. Tom. Ali, Janae W. 2006 & 2013.

We Love Feedback

Send your feedback to
feedback@transitionwhatnow.com

Please consider leaving a review for this book by visiting.
TransitionWhatNow.com

57918616R00098

Made in the USA
Columbia, SC
15 May 2019